WORKING THE SOUL

Reflections on Jungian Psychology

Charles Poncé

North Atlantic Books
Berkeley, California

Working the Soul:
Reflections on Jungian Psychology

Copyright © 1988 by Charles Poncé

ISBN 1-55643-033-7

Published by North Atlantic Books
2320 Blake Street
Berkeley, California 94704

Cover art by Ruth Terrill
Illustrations by Michael Maier, *Atalanta Fugiens*, 1617
Cover and book design by Paula Morrison

Part of this book was first published as *Papers Toward A Radical Metaphysics: Alchemy*, North Atlantic Books, 1983.

Working the Soul: Reflections on Jungian Psychology is sponsored by the Society for the Study of Native Arts and Sciences, a nonprofit educational corporation whose goals are to develop an ecological and crosscultural perspective linking various scientific, social, and artistic fields; to nurture a holistic view of arts, sciences, humanities, and healing; and to publish and distribute literature on the relationship of mind, body, and nature.

CONTENTS

In Praise of Bombast 11

Paracelsus and the Wound 19

Saturn and the Art of Seeing 29

An Alchemical Allegory:
   Notes Toward an Understanding of Genesis 57

Woman, the Feminine, and Alchemy 73

On the Androgyne 91

The Alchemical Light 125

On the Possession of Consciousness 139

Index 179

To My Mother

"Ithaca has given you the beautiful voyage."
Cavafy

ACKNOWLEDGMENTS

"In Praise of Bombast" was a Foreword to the Shambhala Publications Reprint of *The Hermetic and Alchemical Writings of Paracelcus*, in two volumes, (Berkeley, Ca., 1976).

"On the Androgyne" was delivered as a lecture at the *Age of Androgyne Conference* in November 1976 in Chicago.

"Saturn and the Art of Seeing" was delivered as a lecture at the *Astrology and the Helping Professions Conference* in November 1977 in San Francisco. "Paracelsus and the Wound" was delivered as a lecture at the *Astrology and the Healing Arts Conference* in 1979. Both lectures were sponsored by the National Council for Geocosmic Research.

"Woman, the Feminine and Alchemy," and "An Alchemical Allegory" first appeared in *Maitreya* 4 & 5 (1973 & 1974). 'An Alchemical Allegory" also appeared in revised form in *Arche: Notes and Papers on Archaic Studies* (1978). All pieces have been revised for this publication.

I wish to express special thanks to my editor and publisher, Richard Grossinger, for his patience and encouragement.

"Human life is in danger right from the beginning: it is promised neither on an archetypal nor a biological plane. It must come into being of its own material and make its psyche and spirit out of itself, its body. No matter how many transcendental planes there may (or may not) be, we cannot overlook or escape the sheer immensity of creation on a purely physical plane. The alchemists who sought to raise spirit or soul ever out of matter, uncommon substance out of common, and gods themselves out of ashes, understood implicitly that we are bound by our mortality. The decay and pain around us is not the wasting and grief of a mere residual world in which we chanced to occur; it is the decay and pain of us, the fact of our substance. We put on the mortal coil with great difficulty and minute precision; we cannot be abstracted from it, and we cannot idealize our wholeness and mentation as if it were solely angelic or metaphysical. The crisis of our becoming is real, not the image of a higher dimensional realm and not the symbol for another mortality."

—from *Embryogenesis* by Richard Grossinger

PREFACE

The papers that follow were created over a period of ten years either in the form of articles, lectures or introductions to other works. Each of them deals with issues and images central to traditional alchemical concerns. Some approach alchemy from a psychological perspective, others from a mythological, and yet others from a metaphysical. That is, three dialects or voices are employed, each nonetheless of the same language.

None to my way of thinking describes what the new metaphysic might be. Some might hopefully point in a general direction, while others point back in time. I would have liked to have been able to tell you what the new metaphysic might be, but all that I can imagine is that we flounder at the tail end of an aeon whose metaphysic sinks into itself. Mircea Eliade once noted that the speed with which humanity presently attempts to discover its origins might be likened to the old folk-belief that the whole of a person's life flashes before their eyes as they die. Some might find it fanciful to liken civilization to a person — body stretched out through the centuries, history its life, this moment the time of its dying. But there is a certain amount of truth to this image. The historical person is the aeon, the millennium that quickly draws to a close before our eyes. This time dies and all of our modern fears regarding the possibility of the planet's destruction are essentially deep intimations of a death occuring at the collective perimeter of our souls.

History appears to inform us that apocalyptic fears arise at times of great transition. Every such change is at first experienced as a death unless there is available a metaphysic that sees in such endings images of regeneration and rebirth. No such metaphysic appears to be presently available. But alchemy, that metaphysic shelved with the advent of science, the art which strove to transform endings into births (which itself was put to an untimely death because of a misunderstanding) might give us a clue.

It is with such hope that these imaginings are offered.

IN PRAISE OF BOMBAST

"Let him not be another's who can be his own."
Paracelsus

The hard facts concerning the man are as follows: he was born on the shore of Lake Zurich on November 10, 1493 as Philippus Aureolus Theophrastus Bombastus von Hohenheim and was interred in the cemetery of St. Sebastian in Salzburg on September 21, 1541 as Theophrastus Paracelsus. His physician father, Wilhelm von Hohenheim, the bastard son of Georg Bombast of Hohenheim near Stuttgart, Grand Master of the Order of the Knights of St. John, journeyed penniless to Switzerland and settled in the old canton of Schwyz. There, in an inn close by the Devil's Bridge, he met and married Elsa Ochsner, the inn-keeper's daughter who served as a nurse's aid at a nearby hospital. Subject to manic depressive states, she was to leap from the Devil's Bridge into the Siehl River nine years after the birth of Paracelsus. Father and son left shortly afterwards for the outpost of the German Empire, Villach, where Wilhelm became an instructor at a school of mining. It was here where Paracelsus, working as an assistant to his father, first came into contact with alchemy before setting out into the world at the age of fourteen to become the phenomenon that he intrinsically was.

History tells us that the grown Paracelsus was a difficult man, prone to outbursts of invective aimed at the established medical and spiritual authorities of his time. He abhorred untested theory and kicked against the one-sided metaphysical views of his peers with the equally one-sided and abrasive certainty of his experience. During his brief and ill-fated position as Professor at Basle, he invited to his lectures barber-surgeons, alchemists, apothecaries, and others lacking academic background as an expression of his belief that only those who actively practised an art knew it. "The patients are your textbook," he pontificated, "the sickbed is your study," heaping abuse upon the heads of medical students who never saw a patient before their graduation. He ridiculed those who placed more importance on titles than practice and solemnly declared that "if disease put us to the test, all our splendor, title, ring, and name will be as much help as a horse's tail." He was the first to ever lecture in the language of the street, rather than in the official academician's Latin, and the first publicly to condemn the medical authority of Avicenna and Galen, flinging their writings into a bonfire on St. John's day in 1527. As for the renowned Celsus, whose medical theories held sway at the time, he declared that he was (and it was true) better and beyond Celsus — *para-celsus* —. He was run out of Basle.

The conviction of his own experience and practice eventually paid off: he invented chemical urinalysis, chemical therapy, and suggested a biochemical theory of digestion. He demanded that the application of cow dung, feathers, urine and other obnoxious concoctions to wounds be given up in favor of keeping the wounds clean, stating, "If you prevent infection, Nature will heal the wound all by herself." Thus, he anticipated modern techniques of antiseptics by several centuries. In a posthumous treatise on syphilis containing the most comprehensive clinical description the period ever produced, we find that he was the first to perceive that the disease could only be contracted by contact. He was the discoverer of the mercury treatment for the disease as well. Germ theory was anticipated by him in his proposal that diseases were entities in themselves, rather than states of being, that invaded the body to fight with the *archeus* (vital or spiritual force). He therefore gave birth to clinical diagnosis and the administration of highly specific medicines rather than the traditional cure-all remedies of the time. Out of this there also arose the important issue of properly measured dosages for specific ailments. He called for the humane treatment of the mentally ill (but was again ignored for several centuries), seeing in them not creatures possessed by evil spirits but "brothers" ensnared in a treatable malady. Refuting the traditional claim that mental illness was a sin in need of exorcism, he called for a medical approach that concentrated on the treatment of spirit rather than the punishment of body.

He introduced the black hellebore to European pharmacology, prescribing the correct dosage necessary to alleviate certain forms of arteriosclerosis, and recommended the use of iron for "poor blood," emphasizing the importance of employing only the product of plants and not metals. To all of this we can also credit Paracelsus with the creation of the terms "chemistry," "gas," and "alcohol" as well as the discovery of zinc as the active ingredient in the production of brass. And, yes, we can also credit the thorns of his personality for the traditional belief that the word "bombast" was forged by others out of his family name in memory of his irrascibility.

And all of this, along with his numerous writings on practically every area of medical concern (enough to fill two thousand six hundred folio pages of the 1616 edition of his works) was accomplished against the backdrop of an itinerary that would exhaust the most accomplished of modern-day jet-setters: France, Germany, Italy, Denmark, the Netherlands, Sweden, Russia, Spain, England, the Holy Land, Alexandria, the Balkan peninsula, Cyprus, Rhodes, and (as some of his writings appear to indicate) Kos, Samos, and Lesbos. Everywhere he set foot he sought the practitioners of his art at levels of society foreign to the academic world. In time he would become the most accomplished of physicians on the Continent, the lover of the impersonal in humanity: it was the illness in his patients which drew out the vast store of warmth and eros he reserved solely for them. So much for the facts surrounding the human called Paracelsus.

*   *   *

Up until the appearance of the storm called Paracelsus, alchemy and medicine employed the traditional theories of the philosopher Aristotle and the physician Galen. Aristotle's four element theory remains with us today in Astrology, so we need not review its principles here. Besides, it was with Galen that Paracelsus took issue.

Galen had appended to the Aristotelian theory of the elements the Hippocratic doctrine of the four humours believed to be contained within every body: the blood, the phlegm, the yellow bile, and the black bile. These gave rise respectively to the four tempers: the sanguine, phlegmatic, choleric, and the melancholic.

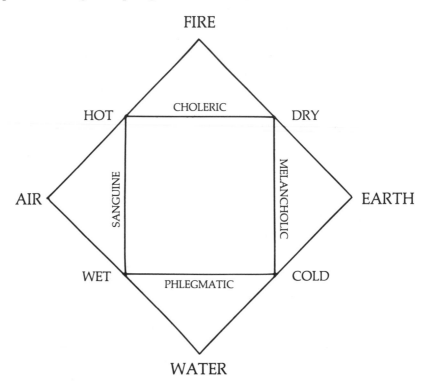

Centuries later the great Arabic alchemist, Jabir ibn Hayyan, further modified the Aristotelian thesis. Whereas Aristotle stated that minerals and fusible metals came into being through the activity of two different smoky and vaporous exhalations, Jabir stated that the two exhalations actually created an intermediary stage governed by Sulphur and Mercury. He held that it was the combination of these two substances in varying degrees that gave rise to metals and minerals. The whole of Western alchemy thereby became grounded in Jabir's theory, until Paracelsus came along.

Jabir's amendments to the Aristotelian element theory did not in any way affect its use in medicine. The Galenic thesis reigned supreme and the introduction of Jabir's emendations served to do nothing more than separate the issue of soul and body. The body was under the reign of the four humours and they in turn were governed by the planets; the soul of the elements, and therefore of the universe, became the concern of the alchemists. True, the planets figured in alchemy, but only in regard to psychic or spiritual realities, not the realities of physical ailments. The Galenic doctors operated under the principle that "contrary cures contrary," and thus administered "dry" remedies for "moist" diseases, cold for hot. These remedies or "Galenicals" as they were called, were primarily created out of herbal concoctions. Obviously, from what we know today concerning the curative power of herbs, they were on to something. Yet, as far as Paracelsus was concerned they were fools and charlatans for they knew nothing of chemical and mineral therapy.

The first thing he did to revolutionize not only medicine but the whole of alchemy as well was to reject the four humour theory and substitute a chemical theory of humours as properties: bitter, sour, salt, and sweet. The body, he insisted, was a chemical system composed of the two alchemical principles sulphur and mercury, to which he added a third principle, salt. In such a manner did the *Tria prima* theory of alchemy appear. Illness arose because of a weakening of the body's defenses brought about by an imbalance of these three principles, thus inviting the *Archei* of disease to invade. The only way to correct this imbalance, Paracelsus insisted, was through the administration of mineral medicines and not the Galenic organic remedies. Thus Paracelsus' entire concern with alchemy was *medicinal* and was quickly to give rise to a branch of alchemists known as iatrochemists — those who solely concerned themselves with the creation of medicines. The rise of iatrochemistry, and of pharmaceutics in general during the seventeenth century, grew directly out of his medical involvement with the theories of alchemy. With one stroke Paracelsus revolutionized centuries of alchemical thought. The difficulties most modern readers have in understanding alchemical texts grows out of this very clear division in the history of alchemical theory. One should ask, with every text published after the sixteenth century, whether or not the basic philosophic stance of the author is Classical or Paracelsian. Then one may safely proceed to other confusing matters.

We therefore have in Paracelsus the reworking of medieval alchemical theory that gave birth to the chemical treatment of physical illness. The man who wrought this change would in time turn to the alchemists from whom he had learned so much and cry, "Don't make gold, make medicines!"

                    *   *   *

The concept of *daemons*, of guiding spirits or voices couched deep within one's heart or mind, is on the whole preposterous to the twentieth century Western intellect. Rather it is easier to believe in the ability to levitate or teleport than to be victim of an interior guiding spirit. But the Greeks knew and respected this type of experience, as did several of the European alchemists. It is a simple phenomenon, we are told, to which one is inherently susceptible from birth, or which can be laboriously induced through religious or philosophic regime. Paracelsus appears to have been in the class of Socrates — born with the blessing, even driven by it beyond himself. One so possessed tends to trample on convention and convictions, rarely looking back to make excuses. What dictates is a spirited passion for understanding, whose back could be broken by the dialect of what passes for reason, intellectual pomp, and the fear of ostracism by one's fellow persons. Wherever Paracelsus discovered the rigidity of the learned holding sway over the fluidity of the soul, he revolted. His impatience with the vapidness of theoreticians time and again caused him the loss of all social standing and scholarly reputation. One wonders, would these gifts of society have fed the fire of his spirit or quenched it? Such questions call to mind the refusal of the learned to gaze through the devil telescope of Galileo, the terror of Copernicus that he would be discovered as having realized a new theory of the universe, the pitiful figure of Spinoza stretched out in penance before the synagogue, his peers trampling both his spirit and convictions. Better to stand up. In the West, tradition is a great Iron Maiden within which one becomes imprisoned at the first sign of argument. Only a Mercurial Fool like Paracelsus knows how to slip through such spikes of indignation.

We have before us in the man called Paracelsus a human become symbol, an intrusion of archetypal powers onto the human stage; a benevolent possession. When such events occur in the life of an individual, it becomes almost impossible to concentrate on merely one facet of their effect on the world. First and foremost, Paracelsus was a physician. Upon closer inspection he was also a magician, psychologist, astrologer, diviner, pharmacist, philosopher, metaphysician, teacher, reformer, and alchemist. Such a personage invariably attracts the spiritual needs of the generation that looks at him. For one generation he will be the Faustian archetypal quack, another the physician, and for ours obviously the alchemist. There is no way of knowing what he will be called three hundred years from now, what facet of his mind will be pertinent for the spirit of the future. For a little over the past one hundred years it is the figure of the alchemist that has called to us. With every reprint or reconsideration of this thinker and imaginer a different issue in alchemy becomes prominent. I would suggest it is the issue of Imagination more than any other that now presses itself upon us.

At a time when the Western world suffers from an impoverishment of Images, visual representations of modalities capable of exciting a soul battered by the inanities of pure empiricism, there appear again now texts emphasizing the phantastic, the supernatural, the Divine, and all that may be called the Imaginal. It is time we return to the source of our spiritual Imagination so that we may again individually discover the Gods and the powers we vainly attempt to have given to us like frail wafers. The degree to which we have lost sight of our own interiority, our innate ability to introspect, may be best understood when we consider that we must now receive instruction from foreign emissaries of the Spirit in humanity. What is natural in psyche has in our culture become unique, occult, and mysterious. After centuries of denying the Soul its expression, the Spirit its manifestation, we become students again. Paracelsus would have spit in our notebooks.

Alchemy was, and may again become, the archetypal language of the soul. It was the receptacle into which many could deposit the seeds of their peculiar imaginal visions of things to come. It is for this reason that we continually trace so many sciences — chemistry, pharmaceutics, psychology, medicine, etc. — back to it. Alchemy was all of these things and none of these things. It was the product of the Soul Imagining. Paracelsus was no doubt aware of this when he wrote "The power of the imagination is a great factor in medicine." He as few others since allowed the full play of Imagination in the vessel of the art called Medicine.

So, Ladies and Gentlemen, I reinvoke the Imaginal writings of Paracelsus, Lover of Illness. May he guide you to your own souls and their spiritual Health. But take care, for he may spatter your gowns in the process.

PARACELSUS AND THE WOUND

"No one needs to care for the course of Saturn: it neither shortens nor lengthens the life of anybody. If Mars is ferocious, it does not follow that Nero was his child; and although Mars and Nero may both have had the same qualities they did not take them from each other. It is an old saying that 'a wise man may rule the stars,' and I believe in that saying — not in the sense in which you take it, but in my own. The stars force nothing into us that we are not willing to take; they incline us to nothing which we do not desire. They are free for themselves, and we are free for ourselves. You believe that one man is more successful in the acquirement of knowledge, another one in the acquisition of power; one obtains riches more easily, and another one fame; and you think that this is caused by the stars; but I believe the cause to be that one man is more apt than another to acquire and to hold certain things, and that this aptitude comes from the spirit. It is absurd to believe that

the stars can make a man. Whatever the stars can do we can do
ourselves, because the wisdom which we obtain from God over-
powers the heaven and rules the stars."[1]

These are the words of the alchemist and physician Paracelsus
who believed that only the doctor who fully understood the
heavens could heal the ills of both the body and the mind.

In this paper I would have liked to, had planned to, offer you a
litany for the subtle body, a sermon on the importance of your seeing through the ego-bound astrology of the modern world, caught
up in the illusion that it is indeed working with the soul. I would
have begun by informing you that Paracelsus wrote that
". . . there remains yet another astrology born of the imagination
of man, superior to all the rest."[2] In other words, it is not the
astrology of the visible world one must pay mind to, but rather the
astrology of the invisible or subtle world where powers reside that
too many of us have either forgotten or fail to give credence to. I
would have begun this work of reclamation by telling you that
Paracelsus believed the stars above us could have absolutely no effect upon the stars contained within us unless an intermediary
realm — what he called "the star in persons" — was brought into full
play. He had written, "Imagination is the star in man," and from
this statement I would have much preferred at my leisure to have
you understand that Paracelsus meant whatever has appearance
also has non-appearance — the subtle, the invisible, and the
unseen; that Paracelsus' view was quite explicit: for everything,
there is an underthing, the hidden other that makes the thing a dynamic principle; that in his understanding it is not the movement
of the planets that affects us, but rather the essence which is contained in the star of imagination, something you cannot chart with
an ephemeris. And I would have concluded with his idea that what
we too often discover in the synchronistic moment — the moment
in which chance has meaning — is nothing more than the outcome
of a short-sighted and limited vision of an imagination without
depth, one that fails to see beyond such synchronicities to the
heart of an imaginal world without end. And I would have finally
punctuated his perception that what one should seek with the aid
of astrology is not the meaning behind events — for meaning is a
human construct, something we create in our attempts to sort our
lives out, to find comfort in the manageable and the reasonable —

but rather the power *in* things which is in itself without meaning.

My final paragraphs would have punctuated that for Paracelsus astrology was a tool employed to tell us not only who and what we are, but that we are — that we should look not continually ahead of ourselves to discover when things will be all right (when I will find the right job, when I will be cured, when I will fall in love, etc.) but that things are right as they appear in each moment and that what the moment brings is right. The task of astrology, as that of any helping or healing profession, is to teach us how to carry each moment elegantly, with dignity, for it is the manner in which we receive ourselves that determines whether we grieve or sing, whether what we hear in ourselves is a cacaphony or a melody, whether in that moment we stumble or we dance. That would have been my final statement, but now I will use it as my starting point, having up to this juncture employed as my front man the genius of Paracelsus to which we still aspire centuries later.

Even as I imagined this paper, its focus shifted because of a realization that while much in modern culture concerns itself with the problem of healing, little attention is given to the image of the wound as a physical reality. Our Western concern with health has tended to become an almost spiritual and fashionable affair. The vehicle of this spiritualization has become our new myth, psychology. What I experience in our countless conferences, workshops, and books on health is a new Evangelic Christianization, an aestheticism of disease that all too often equates healthiness with good psychology, soul with some psychological thing called psyche, almost never addressing itself to the body as the carrier of this precious thing. In this regard we must again listen closely to the alchemist Paracelsus:

"The power of sight does not come from the eye, the power to hear does not come from the ear, nor the power to feel from the nerves; but it is the spirit . . . that sees through the eye, and hears with the ear, and feels by means of the nerves. Wisdom and reason and thought are not contained in the brain, but they belong to the invisible and universal spirit which feels through the heart and thinks by means of the brain. All these powers are contained in the invisible universe, and become manifest through material organs, and the material organs are their representatives, and modify their mode of manifestation according to their material construction, because a perfect manifestation of power can only take place in a perfectly constructed organ, and if the organ is faulty, the manifestation will be imperfect, but not the original power defective."[3] In other words, without the proper attention to the body, neither spirit nor soul can impress nor express themselves upon or through us. Thus, we must seriously concern ourselves with the wound. Rarely do we moderns, and one would expect most ancients, turn to ourselves unless we are ill. Few of us pay attention to the interior happenings of our souls, the workings of our bodies, unless something is not working the right way. What brings me to the psychiatrist or internist's office is the wound. It is by the wound that I eventually arrive at a new awareness of something occuring within me. But attending to the wound, I attend to portions of my body and soul that I have ignored. By attending to the wound, I am directed to the particular. My perception of myself as a wholeness breaks down as I now seek to find my wholeness in the wound itself.

This idea is expressed by Carl Jung in his statement that the gods come to us in our diseases,[4] which tells us that in each wound there is a god or a goddess waiting to be discovered, demanding attention. It appears that we now propitiate the gods through our bodies, for they will be propitiated in one way or another. Our bodies have become sacrificial altars. If I am not willing to experience the deity as it is, as a living reality, then it will force me to experience it in my illness, my body becoming a plane of experience for the archetypal.

But there is a general reluctance to accept this idea: people tend naturally to shy away from that which pains. If you ask a person to reflect on a pain or a wound, their immediate reaction is one either of fear or repugnance. The imagery of the wound is sometimes far more real than the wound. A wound can be either ignored or covered over, but few could see it as a mode of transformation. Thus Jung could write that a "neurosis is by no means a merely negative thing, it is also something positive. . . The neurosis contains the patient's psyche, or at least an essential part of it. . . To lose a neurosis is to find oneself without an object: life loses its point and hence its meaning. This would not be a cure, it would be a regular amputation."[5] Here is a good place to remind you that the root of the word cure was "to care," and that our curing today, in the twentieth century, tends to think only of getting rid of. If, indeed, as Jung suggests, the gods now come to us in our diseases, to cure ourselves in this manner would be to rid ourselves of the gods and goddesses. Thus, it is not enough to treat the wound, tend to the disease, with the intent of ridding ourselves of it. We should instead approach each wound, each illness, as a soul-message, an indication that there is something in ourselves we have refused.

Several recent and popular publications have stressed the belief that we should rid ourselves of the morbidity in disease, assume that the metaphors of illness are something that we have imposed upon our bodies, that to be healthy one must in some mysterious manner be freed from the image of illness. The implication is that if illness could be relieved of the metaphors of illness, of the running sore, the cancerous hole in the lung, the crippled spine, that death would somehow become a glorious experience, that we would see life in a new way. But what of the reality of the stinking wound, the stench of terminal cancer? Are we to deny that this is indeed what happens to the body? How can we escape from this reality?

The refusal to see in illness the dark side, the death side, is ultimately a refusal of the gods. And what exactly is so difficult in allowing that what we have or have not done with our souls in some mysterious fashion does indeed bring us into the presence of the god in our disease? What is the cause of this fear of the dark thing in our body and our psyche? How can we expect to realize the whole of life if we do not accept the life we have received *as a wholeness?*

This consequence is in certain ways expressed in mythological and religious symbolism. The wounded god invariably points toward transformation. The imitation of the Christ is finally an imitation of his wounding, of his experience of transformation through the suffering and pain brought about by the conflict of the opposites within us, the suspension of our lives between the two extreme poles of whatever heaven and earth might symbolize for each of us, where we all sooner or later become nailed, fixed, and suspended. It is neither on earth nor in heaven where we suffer our transformation, but somewhere between the two, in a space none of us would consciously create for ourselves, but that nonetheless is a point of embarkation. We tend to overlook the fact that the term synchronicity refers us to accidents — not just any kind of accident, but what Jung called meaningful coincidences in which inner and outer realities suddenly mesh. The message is contained in the accident, and can therefore be an enlightenment of the most painful sort. A synchronicity is the outcome of two worlds clashing to form a bridge for our perceptions. Thus the image of the suspended Christ is a wounding and an accident of the first order, for it did not merely light up the suffering of the god-man on the cross but has lit up the minds and imaginations of millions over the centuries. It was an accident that occurred in the collective psyche, a synchronicity whose effects have still not yet been fully assimilated. Nor should we forget the symbolism of the exiled and wandering Jew, for, as we have each experienced, the wound and the illness exile us from others, drive us into a state of anxious wondering and wandering. Illness removes us from others initially, in some extreme cases separates us from them forever as in the case of the badly deformed or the perpetually infectious. The wound drives us into ourselves, and it is this that allows us an immediate and intimate contact with our souls — if we are capable of receiving it as a numinous event, an archetypal moment that seeks to make us participants in an eternal happening.

   I call your attention to the two major images given us by the East and the West: those of the Christ and the Buddha. The Buddha is portrayed in a meditative posture, seated, eyes closed, to all appearances oblivious to the world, unmoved and detached. The Christ on the other hand is painfully alert, almost too much so. These images represent two distinct demands of the psyche upon two distinctively unique cultures. The Buddha, in a culture where pain and suffering, death and disfiguration are an everyday reality (to be seen on almost every street corner) is a symbol of transcendence. By him the Easterner is allowed to discover meaning in an all too painful reality, as well as a way to unite the polarities of suffering and non-suffering through transcendence, through a closing-off of the wound's seepage. The Buddha compensates for collective suffering. But in the West, where consciousness has been focused for so long on controlling nature rather than being in it, we find the compensatory figure of the suffering and wounded person. Thus, the soul of a culture encompasses suffering as a way of transformation. And here I do not mean to suggest that we should move through the world with the vision of a masochist, finding in everything a monster of pure delight, but rather that we do not seek to abolish a certain aspect of nature that cannot be denied.

We rebel against an autonomous principle when we find in disease only a just retribution for our sins or divorce illness and suffering from their own stink — hiding the dying away in sanitary resthomes, refusing to speak about pain and illness at cocktail parties, experiencing a sense of failure when we give birth to the retarded, the crippled, the psychotic — we rebel essentially against the autonomy of Nature, the natural breakdown of Nature, the need of Nature to relax into itself, even to collapse into itself in the way that trees retreat into themselves with the advent of Winter. The proof that we retreat from ourselves, from even our bodies, is to be found in the fact that we in the West must today be taught about the process of dying. We have people come to us, professionals, who actually have to tell us that it is all right to die, that dying is a part of a process, and that it is natural.

And in the midst of all this training something even more disastrous is taking place: an unwillingness to accept the possibility that death is final. We never ask ourselves why we fear our endings, why we create psychological and religious eschatologies that assure us of our continuance. We not only fear endings in relationships, jobs, family, but also the ending of the body. And it is this fear of finality that has contributed to a myth in medicine and the healing arts which (when exaggerated) tortures the dying by refusing to let them die. There is in the twentieth century a denial of death, and this denial is blatantly apparent in our demand that we must rid ourselves of that which is sometimes autonomous in Nature — the wound, illness, and death as finality.

Let me turn this notion on its side, open it a bit more for a closer inspection: I am not denying the possibility that there is a continuance of personality after death, but rather exposing that the recent insistence upon the existence of an after-life, an insistence that is not religious in tone but medical and holistic, is only offered as a reason why we should not fear death. I agree that death should not be feared, and that we should be instructed in the reality of death as process. But I find that in all of this insistence on an after-life the body becomes lost. What we focus on is the soul, or the spirit, or the subtle body in the midst of our death, always turning away from what is immediately occuring. We turn away from our bodies in illness and death not because we have resolved the issue of the wound, but because it is far easier to think of an afterlife, far less fearful and painful to surround ourselves with the good feeling that we may not only escape this life in one psychic piece, but that we will no longer have to concern ourselves with our physical humanity.

This approach to death robs us of our tie to Nature, strips us of our humanity in favor of an exquisite angelology of ego. It allows us to slip past the experience of a mystery: that the body is indeed a great temple which moves slowly towards a breakdown and dissolution. The alchemists knew this: that the soul cannot fly, cannot be released from its vessel until the body is broken down, dissolved, and even putrified. When you read the alchemists you will discover that this breakdown and dissolution is the beginning of the Great Work, and that without experiencing and seeing, watching and attending to this momentous operation — keeping the fire of heart and attention at the proper degree — nothing happens. The soul does not fly, the subtle body is not created, nor is the imagination which is the soul's experience of itself opened into eternity. It is this focus on the body and the wound in both life and death that leads to the sacred marriage of the alchemists. Paracelsus stressed, "The eternal is a sign of the dissolution of Nature, and not the beginning of created things, and the end in all things which no nature is without."[6]

In closing I would like to suggest that astrology not simply focus on healing us of life, of moving us away from body into the eternal, secure in our release, but that it remind us that the four elements of astrology referred to the body and not only the mind; that it is not the soul alone which must be healed, but rather as Paracelsus put it, the organs, through which the soul expresses itself. A true medicine and counselling should therefore be one that addresses the immediate, the body of things and the body, for if we really wish to enter into the eternal, see the universe in a grain of sand, we must in our imagination understand that the horoscope is the soul's expression of itself through body, and that woundedness, disease, and the *putrefactio* of our humanity are for us in the West ordained as the focus of a yoga that sees in these sufferings the gods we have rejected.

NOTES

[1]quoted in *Paracelsus: Life and Prophecies,* by Franz Hartmann, M.D., Steiner Books, Blauvelt, New York, 1973, p. 179.

[2]*The Hermetic and Alchemical Writings of Paracelsus,* edited by Arthur Edward Waite, Shambhala, Berkeley, Ca., 1976, vol. II, p. 286.

[3]Hartmann, *op. cit.,* p. 156.

[4]*The Secret of the Golden Flower,* Richard Wilhelm & C. G. Jung, Wehman Bros., New York, 1955, p. 112.

[5]*Collected Works,* C. G. Jung, Princeton University Press, Princeton, New Jersey, Vol. 10, para. 355.

[6]Waite, *op. cit.,* p. 272.

SATURN AND THE ART OF SEEING

The concept of alchemical lead as the stuff that was worked upon in an attempt to create gold is an idea familiar even to the most disinterested. It is in fact often enough used to define the primary concerns of alchemy by those who view this art as having been nothing more than an aberration of early chemistry. A cursory examination of alchemical literature reveals many intelligent and sincere alchemists — the greater majority of whom were physicians — expressing this belief in ways presently obscure to us. The lead they wrote of was not the common lead, no more than was the gold they repeatedly praised.

Their continued reference to Saturn as a synonym for this substance alerts us to the fact that what they spoke of was a particular type of experience rather than a specific substance, and that the lineaments of this experience can be found in the myths of Saturn. This paper will therefore concern itself with the mythological figure of Saturn in the belief that the image of this God at the very least expresses modalities of soul experience common to all of us.

In much the same way that the term "spiritual" limits our appreciation of processes common to our everyday experience, so too does the term "psychological" limit our appreciation of the processes whose mysteries have been reduced to the commonplace. The two terms stand at opposite poles and have come to symbolize viewpoints antagonistic to one another. I therefore prefer to employ the term "archetypal" in the firm belief that it not only defines the activities and conditions referred to by the terms psychological and spiritual, but that it also defines an experience in which the meanings of the two terms can be thought of as indistinguishable from one another. In former ages, a preliminary introduction to a discussion of a God would not have been necessary; nor would the defining of terms have been a prerequisite to such discussions. But we exist at a moment in history where certain phenomena can just as easily be described from a psychological point of view as from a spiritual or religious one. This convergence does not imply, as is more often than not taken to be the case, that one explanation nullifies the other. In fact it points us to the level at which the two perspectives are complementary. If these disciplines simply describe two sides of the same coin, then the coin itself defines a distinct reality in which spiritual and psychological facts simultaneously occur.

Furthermore, whereas psychological and spiritual activities are always described as taking place *in* a clearly defined space — the human mind on the one hand, heaven or the suprapersonal on the other — the archetypes, as Jung has pointed out, "are not found exclusively in the psychic sphere,"[1] but manifest themselves throughout the world. To follow Henry Corbin's lead, the archetype (and the archetypal world) "rather than being situated . . . situates, . . . is situating."[2] To be situated by Saturn, therefore, is to be contained in and working through certain Saturnian modes of being. But we no longer speak in a mythological tongue of experience, and while it is true that "mythology is a psychology of antiquity . . . psychology . . . a mythology of modernity,"[3] we are for the time being stuck with psychological language when describing archetypal experiences. As Jung put it, "Only an unparalleled impoverishment of symbolism could enable us to rediscover the gods as psychic factors, that is, as archetypes of the unconscious."[4] We might append to this that only an impoverishment of imaginal language as well could have caused the creation of psychological language.

Having made these statements about psychological language and implied that spiritual or mystical language no longer carries the weight necessary to engage the sceptic empiricist, I am left with the problem of finding a medium within which I can discuss Saturn. This medium would have to be one in which the impact of the archetype on life could be validated if not immediately experienced and seen. Because archetypes affect both the psychological and spiritual areas of life, and because both of these areas have given birth to the art of counselling in one form or another, I believe it would be best to speak of Saturn from the viewpoint of the counselor. But this type of counselor would have to be a peculiar blend of empiricist and metaphysician, having at his or her disposal a system whose very structure is archetypally given. In addition, the system would have to have as its structural base a clear-cut connection to archetypal images, if not myths themselves, and it would have to derive its information solely from those images or symbols. Furthermore, it could not be recent, with origins far removed from the created ideographic realm of modern persons. In short, its authority would have to be a given, derived in much the manner that an archetype expresses itself. Admittedly, these qualifications could in part answer certain schools of psychological thought, and almost all religious counselling. But neither one of these forms of counselling rely solely on the archetypes for seeing. Both demand that a human story be told, each then seeking to fit that story within the mold of the image they believe the story fits. And, furthermore, neither one of them can claim to see an entire life as an archetypal structure which from moment to moment is effected by archetypes that can be specifically named. Finally, neither one can claim a long and intimate connection with the art by which imagined realities could be revealed and worked upon: the art of alchemy.

The form of counselling that appears to fit all of the above requirements is astrology. I cannot here argue the reasons why astrology does indeed work,[5] but must ask my reader at least to allow that as a counselling tool it can be as effective as any other. I will therefore speak of it as an art that still affords us the greatest possibility for speaking an archetypal language that includes both psychological and spiritual perspectives.

*   *   *

The most familiar description of Kronus is given us in Hesiod's creation myth, the *Theogony*. The tale informs us that the Great Mother, Gaia, came into being first and created the limits of the known world, along with the Titans, Cyclopes, and her own brother-husband, Uranos. Uranos came to her daily for sexual union, refusing to allow the children born of these unions to issue from her body. She in time grew weary of his sexual demands along with the burden of her imprisoned children. Petitioning her children to aid her in her plight, Kronos came forth armed with a sickle given him by his mother and emasculated his father, tossing the severed genitals into the ocean. Kronos then took over rulership and fathered the pantheon that would in time rule the world: Zeus, Hera, Poseidon, Demeter, Hestia, and Hades. Warned that one of his children would supplant him, he took to swallowing them as soon as they were born. His wife, Rhea, tiring of her husband's demands, hid the infant Zeus from his father. Once grown, Zeus battled with Kronos for the throne and after successfully defeating him banished the old ruler to Tartaros, a dark region believed to be beneath Hades itself, so distant that an anvil dropped from the surface of the earth would fall for nine days before reaching his father's final prison.

The manner by which Kronos was defeated is worth considering. Zeus asked the Titaness, Metis (Wise Council or Insight), to aid him in the administration of an emetic to his father. After swallowing, Kronos vomited up Zeus' brothers and sisters — the Olympians who from that time forward would reign from above, if not from the sky itself.

What we are more than likely witness to in this particular tale is the personification of the type of shift in consciousness that occurs anytime a culture moves from a meteorologically-based calendar to one purely astronomical. One could here phantasize that the seasonal calendar, in that it grew out of simple observations of the immediately felt cycles of change occurring in Nature, gave rise to the myths of the Great Mother and her dying and resurrecting consorts. More than likely the initial calendric myths would have arisen from the simple movements of the Sun and Moon. With more detailed observation of these two bodies the shift from a seasonal to an astronomical calendar began to occur. A meteorological calendar demands nothing more than simple observation. The cycle of the seasons signifies when to plant, when to harvest, when to store up provisions. That is, consciousness need little exert itself; need do nothing more than attend to what is happening before one's eyes and upon the land. The shift towards a calendar founded upon astronomical events would have demanded not only a focusing of attention on phenomena removed from one's immediate perception, but the creation of a notational system as complex as the movements it recorded. The sudden emergence of sky gods where once earth goddesses reigned probably mirrors such an event. This new type of attention, this honing of a consciousness that once attended only to the immediacy of phenomena, was the seed of abstract and philosophical thought.

Furthermore, the tendency of the deep psyche to personify phenomena, that same tendency which originally allowed the earth to be seen and experienced as female, as Great Mother, continued in its propensity, now identifying the sky with the Great Father and the male. Thus, this shift into a new modality of consciousness at first not only became identified with the masculine but would in time become a synonym for consciousness. Such personifications still exist and are the very stuff of those psychological theories that personify the realms now called consciousness and the unconscious. We therefore find Freud writing that the "motive force of repression in each individual is a struggle between the two sexual characters. The dominant sex of the person, that which is the more strongly developed, has repressed the mental representation of the subordinated sex into the unconscious. Therefore the nucleus of the unconscious (that is to say, the repressed) is in each human being that side of him which belongs to the opposite sex. . . . To put the theory briefly: with men, what is unconscious and repressed can be reduced to feminine instinctual impulses; and conversely with women."[6]

One is forced to ask what exactly is a feminine instinctual impulse, and what a masculine? Is Freud saying that what is repressed in a male, what the ego cannot bear, *becomes* identified as feminine, in a woman masculine? That is, does the very existence of the thing called feminine or masculine depend upon experiences or material that consciousness has denied, has repressed? Is the term "feminine" assigned by a male to a thing he cannot allow of himself, "masculine" that which a woman cannot — and is what each cannot allow solely dictated by social convention, or is it a deep innate propensity to project onto a distinctly other being what is negatively experienced in them? Do our concepts of the masculine and the feminine come into existence through repression first, and then by projection?

Let me come at it from another direction: *whatever* an individual finds intolerable to their psychic stability, is that the stuff that they then project onto the opposite sex? Is the concept of the masculine and the feminine a myth, a projection, nothing more than the display of the deep psyche's tendency to personify? And does such personification demand images of extreme difference, creating self by hostility to an imagined other? Listen to the psychological imaginings of the Jungian Erich Neumann:

> Consciousness . . . is masculine even in women, just as the unconscious is feminine in men . . . it is consistent with the conscious-unconscious structure of the opposites that the unconscious should be regarded as predominantly feminine, and consciousness as predominantly masculine. This correlation is self-evident, because the unconscious, alike in its capacity to bring to birth and to destroy through absorption, has feminine affinities. The feminine is conceived mythologically under the aspect of this archetype; uroboros and Great Mother are both feminine dominants, and all the psychic constellations over which they rule are under the dominance of the unconscious. Conversely, its opposite, the system of ego consciousness, is masculine. With it are associated the qualities of volition, decision, and activity as contrasted with the determinism and blind 'drives' of the preconscious, egoless state."[7]

Here we are told that the feminine is that which creates and destroys, blind, without ego, and compelled; masculine, that which is decisive, volatile, active and in control. Whereas in Freud the qualities of the feminine and the masculine are determined by their repression, here in Neumann's mythology neither male nor female would want anything to do with the feminine. Is this not the stuff of Hesiodic, Kronian mythology? What is "self-evident" to Neumann is that the unconscious is blind and that the thing called ego is no different from its forerunner in our myth of Kronos.

Both Freud and Neumann reveal personifications of the first

order. Jung, in attempting to clarify the matter towards the end of his life, corrects his original position, the one from which Neumann took his lead, by stating that by identifying "Sol with consciousness and Luna with the unconscious, we would now be driven to the conclusion that a woman cannot possess a consciousness."[8] He goes on to say, "The error in our formulation lies in the fact, firstly, that we equated the moon with the unconscious as such, whereas the equation is true chiefly of the unconscious in man; and secondly, that we overlooked the fact that the moon is not only dark but is also a giver of light and can therefore represent consciousness. This is indeed so in the case of woman: her consciousness has a lunar rather than a solar character."[9]

Here too, while nonetheless carried by a more democratic phantasy, the personifying character of the psyche is present, for we are at the same time informed that this lunar character "does not show up objects in all their pitiless discreteness and separateness, like the harsh, glaring light of day, but blends in a deceptive shimmer the near and the far, magically transforming little things into big things, high into low, softening all colour into a bluish haze, and blending the nocturnal landscape into an unsuspected unity."[10]

So, here we are told that the feminine, or at least the consciousness of women, is a dim light that *deceptively* merges the differences of opposites into a unity, somehow temporarily relieving us of the real essence of objects. As in the myth of Ge and Uranus, Rhea and Kronos, the feminine is deceptive, a betrayer. And the masculine? An over-bearing nit-picker. Psychology is as subject to these personifying qualities of deep psyche as the old mythology. No matter how far along this road of consciousness we may continually pride ourselves in having advanced, we are left with the bothersome possibility that every perception, every insight, will in time (as history has shown) be discovered to have to some degree been riveted with projections. This is what Jung meant when he said that the unconscious is inexhaustible: the base of the human soul, for want of another phrase, is *potentia* — a tree of eternal life comprised of our continued need to know, to understand, to be certain. And here we see why a symbol contains all the information needed for its decipherment, why nothing need be added to the image, for the image, whether it be presented by a mythographer from the fifth century B.C. or the twentieth century

A.D., carries with it every imaginable hook needed for any human projection. It is by such hooks, through such engagements, that we strive to free ourselves from the personifying tendencies of the soul—tendencies that ultimately give shape to a thing we call the unconscious.

To return to our opening description of the theogonic myth, we have in the figure of Kronos the cast of liberator first, devourer second, and vanquished third. We also have in the name Kronos the idea that the God creates time divisions—he delineates beginning, middle and end. Thus, every Kronos time has these three qualities. Whereas Uranos knew no limit but continually set about the business of creation without end, Kronos brings a close to eternal creation. In short, he constitutes the first phenomenon peculiar to being in this world. He is the father of our experience *in* being. When I am pressed for time, fear its loss, suffer its interminable passage, wonder where it went, then I know the full meaning of Kronos as an oppressive power. Kronos limits and therefore defines the experience of life, thus he becomes the archetype of history. Kronos destroys the creative principle of the father in order to liberate. We might psychologize this and say that my cutting free of the constraining influence of father at the parental and societal level allows those qualities that I was born with to come into the light of day, into consciousness.

Murray Stein has pointed out that this Creation tale corrects the Freudian supposition that the male child fears castration by the father.[11] Here, it is quite simply indicated that it is the father who fears castration by the son. Castration is de-meaning, a depowering that leads to the father's fall. This re-sighting of the Freudian myth of Oedipus leads to some startling implications.

Freud informs us that it is the young male's fear of castration that leads to an initial experience of guilt, which in turn gives rise to the establishment of the super-ego—a structure created by the internalization of the father principle contained in both the real father and society. With the image of the castrating son instead of the Freudian castrating father, castration becomes a vehicle for the establishment of the young Heroic ego. Here, Saturn becomes a creator or liberator of a new form of consciousness, a consciousness that sets a limit upon the fecundity of the primal psyche we carry within. It stops the psyche's original desire, easily witnessed in young children, to act on impulse, even compulsively. Kronos/

Saturn is the element that halts play, teaching the child that there must be a limit to the desire to fulfill its pleasures in every given moment. Thus, Kronos symbolizes the quality in consciousness that is capable of interrupting, suppressing, repressing, and re-directing the spontaneous and instinctual. And it does this for the purpose of meeting and maintaining the demand for order that is peculiar to the human experience. I refer to this as Spiritualization, defining the process as the limiting effect of ego on that which is without ego or non-ego.

The next image that the tale of Kronos presents is the son be-coming the father: no sooner am I freed of that which parents and constrains me than I become parent and constrainer. I then devour my own children, my own creativity and potential, and even my own future. Kronos is one who would turn every experience into a father-experience, allowing no change of rules, always telling us that the right way to go about things has been left us by the past. Kronos is against materia, against body, against nature. He is the defining spirit of an age, of the time, of the moment.

Psychologically, the entire myth reads as follows: Uranos, the sky, would keep or locate all creative potentials in matter, the stuff of the world. It would seek to materialize and concretize every new idea. It would take every spontaneous creative thought and make it practical and earthbound. It would accomplish this through perpetual penetration of earthly matters and concerns, re-fusing to let go of its mater/matter. Kronos frees such potential by castration. So is the psyche ensnared in the tendency to materialize or literalize, freed up and allowed to come into the light of day. But now this creative energy, having seen the light of conscious-ness, becomes ensnared in Kronos—by the limits of spirit-ualization. Its function now is to nourish spirit, the paternal, dogma, institutions, and ego. What eventually releases the con-straining power of this Saturnian energy is insight, the application of Metis. That is, by in-sighting, by penetrating to the belly of the archetype, we liberate the powers it imprisons.

Everything that I have presented up to this point concerning Kronos fits within parameters of both psychology and astrology. It is at just this point where one is tempted to make of the two arts one, to in fact relate the Kronos figure of mythology to the psych-ology of C.G. Jung, in particular to the structure and dynamics of the human psyche. However, to do so would be to ignore the fact that Jung himself stated that the archetypes transcend the human psyche, an idea more in accord with the ancient theories of astrology than the modern attempt to legitimize astrology by turning it into a psychology, a *science* of soul rather than an *art*. This drive towards "scientific" respectability on the part of astrology — a drive that psychology itself became victim to not too long ago — serves to do nothing more than deprecate valuable ideas that astrology originally held. What we fail to see in such an effort is that if in making a thing respectable we must divorce ourselves from the past then we become the castrating Kronos ourselves on the one hand, and the devourer of all that is potential in soul on the other. And here I specifically refer to the fact that the planets of astrology were once understood as Gods — not psychological co-ordinates. Our present inability to accept such an idea grows out of our failure to experience myth.

Simply put, myth refers us to a dimension residing beside and beyond the lineaments of what we usually identify as reality. It was once the tale of the Gods, of powers whose phantastic and improbable natures when viewed through the rationalism of the twentieth century, could only exist, if they exist at all, in imagination. We think of myth as something antiquity has left us, of something once believed in but no longer tenable. Myth more often than not is deemed little more than the fancy shadow of what was once considered a reality. We today in the West pride ourselves in knowing that it is certain atmospheric conditions that give cause to thunder and lightning, not the great God Zeus; that what causes panic or hysteria is a psychological difficulty and not the God Pan; that love simply comes about because of a series of mutual attractions and compatibilities, and not the God Eros. When we look at myth we see it as nothing more than a system of metaphors pacifying the scientific ignorance of our ancestors.

What we fail to appreciate concerning these ancestors and their myths is the immediacy of the phenomena portrayed. The image of Zeus was not created in an attempt to explain thunder and lightning, but rather was the spontaneous representation of an emotional response to thunder and lightning. To see myth as nothing more than a series of metaphors is to assume that myth is a logical construct, a product of pure intellect. Myth alludes to the affect accompanying a specific reality which in the final analysis is undecipherable except in terms of the image. Myth, if nothing else, is the record of an unreferable experience.

The experiences that gave birth to these mythic images still occur, but today we have a different set of terms to define them — transpersonal or transcendent, altered states of consciousness, hypnogogic, or hallucinatory. What is of interest in all of these is that they distance us from such experiences by locating them in a realm outside or above so-called normal consciousness. But what we today call "normal consciousness" is actually a quality of perception defined by the influence of logical positivism or empiricism. We forget that we are not born empiricists but trained to perceive and experience reality from such a vantage point. While an empirical approach to the phenomenal world is critical for the differentiation and classification of phenomena, when it is used to define our immediate and felt experience the danger of splitting ourselves off from the other dynamic factors of the soul becomes very real. This type of thinking leads to the creation of ego-psychologies that seek to standardize human experience.

But if we remind ourselves of what Jung said concerning the archetypes — that they pass through, include and affect soul, but are not its property — then we are left with the fact that the archetypes not only work on something else, but also perform this work *somewhere else*. The first and most apparent place is in nature itself. The other place we shall speak of shortly. What all of this implies is that the person is not the center of the cosmos: that the person is, in fact, something that must be connected to the cosmos. What psychology presently attempts to do, and I suspect much of astrological counseling, is to separate the person from the cosmos by insisting that consciousness is the significator of an ultimate reality.

This humanizing of the archetypes in both psychology and astrology becomes blatantly apparent when we turn to the concept of soul. Invariably, we speak of "my soul," ignoring the fact that early philosophy spoke of "the soul," or the *anima mundi* or world soul. It was believed that the entire universe was contained in such a soul, and that we were each allotted a small portion of that larger soul to work upon in our lives. But where in either psychology or astrology is there work done on the world soul? Nowhere that I can see. And where in either psychology or astrology do we not relate soul to life, earthly life, my life, the life of the individual and of persons? In short, what has happened to *this* archetype? Obviously, in attending to the problem of making lives astrological and psychological, we have cut ourselves off from what is fully archetypal.

We might arrive at a clearer picture of this original soul principle if we turn to the zodiacal figure of astrology—that figure which portrays the ideal relationship of the elements, signs, houses and planets to each other. This zodiacal figure is what was once referred to as the world soul, or the grand person. What is curious about this figure is that no human being alive in either past, present or future could ever have a horoscope like it. That is, my horoscope fails to hit the mark of archetypal wholeness, revealing where I have fallen short of this wholeness. Because this zodiacal figure, or archetype of wholeness, always lurks behind every horoscope, astrological counseling becomes an attempt to perform the impossible: to lead the person in the direction of this wholeness. Psychology does much the same with its concept of "normalcy" or wholeness.

In astrology, the natal chart (in psychology the circumstances of life) becomes the focus of attention. Both types of data are employed in an attempt to regulate or normalize the individual. In each instance the attempt is to see what the problem in an individual life is, and how it can either be corrected or compensated. In astrology, therefore, we find ourselves dealing with two dimensions. The first is that depicted in the natal chart: the given of a life, that is to say, the particulars of my history. The second is the psychological: to what degree the physical realities have impaired or enhanced my psychology. Where is the blockage and where is the flow? The theory of the archetypes can be very helpful here, for we often point to exactly how and when I have been affected by an archetype—but it is limited, for it leaves out a third dimension of the person.

This dimension appears to have been forgotten by both astrology on the whole, and psychology in part, and is what the alchemist Paracelsus referred to when he wrote that there is a double system of stars. There are the stars without and the stars within. In order for the outward Saturn to have any effect on me, it must work through the inner Saturn.[12] Paracelsus adds that between the two star systems there exists a medium star zone—thus his famous dictum that "Imagination is the star in man." It is through the medium of imagination that we are capable of bringing forth a new heaven.[13] In another work he informs us that "he which would perfect this art [alchemy] must, as it were, build a new world."[14] In other words, in order to create the Philosopher's Stone, one first must create a new world through the use of imagination.

If we read the alchemists carefully, especially the papers collected by Elias Ashmole in his *Theatrum Chemicum Britannicum*, it becomes clear that this Philosopher's Stone comes into being by following an astrological schedule and that the Stone answers the description of the zodiacal archetype, the *anima mundi*, or perfect person. Thus, the astrological wholeness imaged by the zodiacal archetype can be created by an individual: it is apparent what is being alluded to here is the subtle body. It is just here that things start to become difficult for us in the modern world, for what is being suggested is that we can create an ephemeral body, a personality capable of existing after the body's death. In addition, this body is created out of no-thing, out of air to all appearances, and it has an independent life of its own both in and out of human existence. Before we scoff at this idea, it would do us well to consider some modern theories of psychology.

A case in point is the theory of the ego. Psychology in general agrees that the ego is not a given — it is not fully present in the infant — but a thing created over the course of the years. In time it becomes the center of consciousness, even identified with consciousness. There is no denying that a psychic substance has been made, created, out of no-thing. This ephemeral body is the child of all western psychologies.

Jung, the creator of the psychological term "complex," has pointed out that the ego is a complex, a complex being defined as a grouping of psychic elements about emotionally toned-contents, a nuclear psychic element around which associations cluster. The term is most familiar to us in such phrases as "mother-complex" or "father-complex," referring us to psychological states in which an individual is engaged or identified with the parent in question to the point where it is detrimental to his or her autonomy as an individual. The ego, being but one of many complexes, may also offer such dangers as can be seen in individuals one would label as being "egotistical." The peculiar feature of complexes that are unconscious, beyond the immediate and willed reach of consciousness, is that they may each form a personality of their own. A complex,

Jung tells us, is a sort of body that can upset the stomach, breathing, and the heart. He likens a complex to a partial personality, pointing out that it is the source of those personalities that appear in schizophrenia.[15]

The picture that we have to this point is of a field of consciousness containing at an idealized center a created psychic body or complex, called the ego. This picture on the other hand tells us that in the unconscious there are any number of other complexes possible — each having an independent life of its own. The ego and these other complexes appear to be spontaneous phenomena. They *happen to us.* Psychology has shown that we can work on these complexes, especially the ego — that a certain amount of willing and attention can alter their basic natures.

Now let me propose this: if it is possible for us to create greater and more substantial properties of this ephemeral thing called the ego, is there not the possibility that we can also create yet another psychic body? And may not this psychic body or complex be the very thing that the ancients and the alchemists referred to as the subtle body of the Stone? If we can create another psychic body, similar in substance and composition to the ego, where then would it reside? One is tempted to equate the place where such a subtle body might take shape as the unconscious itself. But it must be noted that the heaven Paracelsus speaks of is created by imagination: that is, it is something created by the person. The unconscious exists, *it is,* there is no need for us to create it. This other dimension or level or place is composed of imagination and imaginal substances. It is *the* imaginal. This is the dimension of the horoscope, I propose, that has been forgotten: this is the place where the world soul exists, the place where I can become re-connected with the cosmos. Whereas our psychologies tell us we must work on consciousness, ego, and the unconscious, this place need not be worked on. It need only be attended to, allowed admittance into our lives. What happens at this third dimension of the horoscope happens outside of the space/time continuum. It is an archetypal dimension, a place of powers existing beyond the human. The home of the Gods, if you will.

What I am suggesting here is that we are affected by a dimension that has nothing to do with personality development, ego growth, or the expansion of consciousness. What it has to do with is connections, archetypal connections. In both astrology and psychology there is an attitude that one must be strengthened, made better, developed. So we take what we are and we attempt to transform ourselves, become better, whole, palpable. But, I ask you, is there the possibility that what has been given *is* something of value in its own right. And is there the possibility that my experience of archetypal or astrological wholeness might be possible at this imaginal level? We are continually attempting to fit the zodiacal archetype at the personal level — something that is an impossibility — but might not this other dimension of psyche be the very place where it is achieved?

Let me define these three dimensions before moving on: the first would be the place where physical adjustments are made to what has been given; the second would refer us to the psychological work and adjustment that must be made to what is given; and the third would be working on what I am as *given*, without any attempt to alter or modify. The work of this last dimension is an imaginal work. The involvement with what has been given is the stuff of souls. I change nothing, attempt to make nothing better, but perceive "it" as it is in the hope of discerning in it an archetypal meaning that will deepen my perception of life. This would imply that one of the functions of astrology (as well as of psychology) would be involved not with the art of counseling but with the art of seeing, or with the art of revealing — for no other purpose than to see myself clearly as I am. The objective would be not to correct, but literally to objectify; not to expand but to deepen. What is now counseling would become witnessing. The astrologer and the psychologist would aid me in the problem of discovering what I am. Transformation would be discussed not in terms of making something better out of what one has, but in being what one is.

In his book *Re-Visioning Psychology*, James Hillman has defined soul as "a perspective rather than a substance, a viewpoint toward things rather than a thing itself. This perspective is reflective, it mediates events and makes differences between ourselves and everything that happens. Between us and the events, between the doer and the deed, there is a reflective moment — and the soul-making means differentiating this middle ground."[16] The middle ground Hillman refers us to is the medium of imagination that for Paracelsus exists between the stars above and the stars within. It is by differentiating this middle ground, this imaginal dimension, that one connects oneself with nature and the cosmos. Our next question is, how is this to be done? What is the method of soul-making, or reconnecting?

Jung re-discovered one way we might become again engaged, actively, with the archetypal realm. He called this active imagination; it is a short-cut to the unconscious, which entails "the releasing of unconscious processes and letting them come into the conscious mind in the form of fantasies . . ." not "giving priority to understanding" them.[17] Libido, or psychic energy, can only be consciously apprehended and joined to consciousness through the image.[18] The objective of this technique was the bringing over of so-called inferior functions into consciousness for the purpose of transforming them, thus enhancing consciousness. In yet another paper he informs us that psychic processes might be thought of as a scale along which consciousness slides.[19] He likens one end of the scale to the pure instinctual impulse, the other to the image of that impulse or the archetype. To come into contact with the image or archetype, rather than to fall into the compulsive area of the instinct, one need only perform active imagination. In other words, the image is father of the action. Hillman writes that "any transformation of the images affects the patterns of behavior."[20]

The purpose behind the method of active imagination, originally, was that of creating a greater field of consciousness, or bringing things over from the archetypal realm into consciousness. But there is a new suggestion in Jungian psychology that states we must go beyond active imagination into archetypal imagination. The thesis behind this is that active imagination—a process that demands the person performing the imagination include themselves in the images produced, guiding and entering them as they develop—limits the experience of the archetypal or imaginal. What we get ultimately is the story of the imaginer himself. The focus of archetypal imagination would be nothing less than a rooting in that which is beyond psyche, that which the ancients referred to as heaven.[21]

Jung wrote that active imagination in time produces a third thing, "a living birth that leads to a new level of being, a new situation."[22] This is the new world or body that the ancients and the alchemists told us we are capable of forming. By creating this new thing, we truly participate in the work of nature, we somehow affect nature and transform it, making of it not an evolutionary phenomenon, but a revolutionary happening.

I have led you down this road in an attempt to shed light on my statement that the purpose of engaging with the imaginal realm, the archetypal reality, is to become active participants in the transformation of nature. Not *our* natures, but nature itself. This is the real meaning of transformation — it is not person-centered, it is archetypally centered and it is a way in which we may all contribute to the ever-unfolding work of Genesis. The materials of the ancient art of astrology constitute a method by which this may be achieved. In addition to the counselling that the horoscope appears to engender, there is this third work that every astrologer should concern himself with: working with the *image* of the horoscope itself.

My horoscope shows me exactly where and how the imaginal has become enmeshed with me, where the gods have taken on new characteristics, new problems. My horoscope is the continuation of written myth, it is the tale not only of myself, but of the Gods in their evolution in imaginal time and space, their individuation.

The horoscope might therefore be thought of as an active imagination performed by the Gods, or the planets, or whatever you wish to call these powers that shape us. The new function of the astrologer would be to engage me at this archetypal level by having me perform an archetypal imagination on my horoscope. This would entail not an hour of understanding or interpretation, but an hour of story-telling. The astrologer would tell me the story of the particular God-planets, and then point out exactly where my horoscope coincides with the original tale. Then we, the two of us, would engage in a conversation outlining the development of the myths as revealed by the differences in my horoscope. The horoscope would become not just a tool through which I understand myself, but a method by which I can see myself as a part of a larger whole. Instead of a broadening and enlargement of consciousness, this would be a deepening and engagement with soul.

The corpus of texts known as the *Hermetica* has the following:

> Leap clear of all that is corporeal, and make yourself grow to a like expanse with that greatness which is beyond all measure: rise above all time, and become eternal: then you will apprehend God. Think that for you too nothing is impossible: deem that you too are immortal, and that you are able to grasp all things in your thought . . . find you a home in the haunts of every living

creature: make yourself higher than all heights, and lower than
all depths: bring together in yourself all opposites of quality,
heat and cold, dryness and fluidity; think that you are everywhere at once, grasp in your thought all this at once, all times
and places, all substances and qualities and magnitudes
together: then you can apprehend God."[23]

This clearly refers us to the art of archetypal imagination. The
horoscope of the individual is the rocket that allows the person access to this other dimension of experience. The images contained
therein are not just psychological qualities, but the Gods themselves as they exist at the periphery of the human world. The horoscope is a field of imagination and reflection not only through
which we see ourselves, but by which we see *through* ourselves to
the archetypal ground that has created this dance we call life.

Now I must turn you to the next question. What is it that
caused us to lose sight of this level of astrological work? Why have
we failed to see that the horoscope is not only a way into ourselves, but a way out of ourselves as well, into the greater drama
we all carry about or are carried about in? The answer, to my way
of thinking, is the God Saturn.

Consider this: the restraining and repressing of the children by
Uranos might be likened to the early stages of primacy when the
elements that will in time compose the ego are refused light of day.
Assuredly, these are primitive aspects of ego—the monsters of
childhood imagination. Saturn at first releases these elements from
the belly of the unconscious, only in time to devour the newer and
controlling aspects of ego in the form of his children. Everything in
consciousness now becomes spiritualized and controlled. If these
elements are to have any expression at all, it must be through the
father, through paternal law. The new heaven, Olympus, can
come into being only through the release of these children who will
in time rule the world. I suggest here that the new heaven, the
Olympus, is the imaginal heaven of Paracelsus, the reflective
ground of soul that Hillman refers us to, and the deeper level of the
horoscope. The only thing that will allow us to create this heaven
in both astrology and psychology is the application of an elixir by
in-sight. In short, the only way we can release ourselves from
Saturn's tendency to spiritualize and intellectualize the cosmos and
the imaginal is by in-sighting, or seeing into the imaginal through
the mirror of the horoscope.

If there is any one idea I am trying to put forward, it is that we must resuscitate a forgotten function of astrology that allows the reunion of the person with the imaginal, the creation of a subtle body, and the continuance of Genesis. All of this may be accomplished by the re-instatement of a way of seeing with the eyes of the soul.

We must delve deeper into the tale of Kronos, filling out the little details. To begin with, the Uranian difficulty is one that directs all energy into creating stuff from mater — from materia — and filling matter up. Uranian consciousness is a *participation mystique* with the world and with matter. It is a limited consciousness in that it sees nothing but what lies in front of it. The next stage in the development of consciousness is marshalled in by Kronos. He liberates through curtailment of the instinctual and the impulsive.

Kronos then imposes limitations upon his own children by swallowing them. That is, he does not let them remain in matter. He allows the creative issue of his seed into the light of day for a moment before incorporating them in his own body. Instead of a consciousness that works through the body of materia/mother, a making of the world, we now have a consciousness that spiritualizes or intellectualizes the world as well as the instincts or impulses. If energy is to express itself, it must do so in a controlled manner. Kronos is a consciousness that has no contact with either the unconscious or the instinctual. Every impulse, and therefore every creative upsurge, becomes swallowed up.

At first, the containment of all these children appears to be nothing more than a legitimate limitation of things. We today tend to admire the Kronos figure operating in this manner. We say limitation is a necessary quality of life, a function of a good ego. To become whole is to become aware consciously of one's limitations. It is just here where astrological and psychological counselling can itself become Saturnian: by turning all patterns of behavior that do not fit the archetypal model of wholeness into vehicles of transformation; in whatever is difficult or unsavory, we must somehow find something good, and in order to create the good we must obviously have some kind of model of the good. This is the process of spiritualization that Kronos/Saturn adores.

We have already noted Jung's perception that whereas modern persons do not have direct communication with the Gods, the Gods now manifest themselves to us through our illnesses — be such illness physical or psychological.[24] He writes elsewhere that whenever he was confronted with a crisis or major difficulty in life, he invariably found God behind it all. Therefore, to cure ourselves of our illness or our difficulties, to make of the dark stuff of life good stuff and healthiness, is also to rid ourselves of the God in the darkness. To take the difficult image of Kronos/Saturn and manage to find in his demands goodness and reasonableness, is to never know Saturn *as he is*. What we end up knowing is his effect, his mercurial, tricksterish process of spiritualization. This is how Saturn limits us: by not allowing us to experience him as he is. There is a darkness to this god, and he cannot be experienced without it.

The function of Kronos/Saturn is to instruct us in the nature of limitation, depression, and the dryness of a wisdom that seeks to make all things equal. Dryness is the nature of ego, but Heraclitus tells us that, "It is delight, or rather death, to souls to become wet . . ."[25] and that "to souls, it is death to become water: to water it is death to become earth, from earth comes water, and from water, soul."[26] The dry wisdom of the wise old man Saturn is soul become spirit. As Heraclitus points out, it is death to water (soul) to become earth, to become the psychological matter of consciousness and the ego. But life is earth become water, for from water comes soul.

This is a loaded statement when we compare it to the castration in our tale. Uranos, the one totally and purely involved in mater/matter, has his genitals thrown into the ocean by his son Kronos. Hesiod informs us that the castrated member floats upon the ocean for a long time, foam gathering about it, bearing inside it the immortal being who shall soon be spawned—Aphrodite, goddess of love, the "foam born." So it begins: the compulsive sexual engagement of Uranos with his wife Gaia, when prevented—when cut off—leads to the birth of love. Note that it is not sexuality and love that are equated here. What is implied is that behind every compulsive act, there is a seed of love that can emerge if one can cut oneself off from impulsivity.

What is it that accomplishes the end of compulsion? It is this: the limitation of Kronos, the demand that we do not concretize and make physical certain deep inner promptings. What is born of water and defunct genitals is the first image of soul. The message is: the way to soul comes only after putting an end to the concretizing of instinct and the casting of all our energy "out there" into the world. But Kronos does not see or know of this, for Hesiod tells us that he threw his father's genitals behind him, over his shoulder. In short, he failed to see the value concealed in both instinct and compulsion. This is the stuff that Kronos limits by keeping his children away from the feminine, in his own body.

Therefore, the counsellor working with the image of Kronos is faced with two dangers. The first is in not fully appreciating that the limiting effect of Kronos on compulsions and instincts is only good in and for itself if one looks behind the God. The second danger is in failing to see that this statement refers to the physical level alone. In the imaginal realm, at the deepest level of soul, we must experience Kronian blindness if we are to experience love. It is only because Kronos does not see what is contained in the genitals of his father that Aphrodite is born. If he had seen it, he more than likely would have spiritualized the event, making of Aphrodite a Virgin Mary, which she is far from being.

Lucretius, in his work *On the Nature of Things*, informs us that Aphrodite is always accompanied by wild beasts in hot desire. She is the mistress of Ares (Mars in astrology), the God of war, the first being to be tried for murder. Thus, Aphrodite is joined with murderous passion. In that she is the mother of Phobos (fear) and Deimos (terror), it is also implied that every act of love is capable of producing these experiences. As for the god who is her legal husband, Hephaestus, he is a lame blacksmith whom the Gods found comical — his feet were turned backwards. All of which is to say that Aphrodite's divinity is compensated for by that which is *crippled*. In addition, she worried her husband with numerous affairs — another way of saying that in every loving there is the potential for deceit. This is no valentine-card goddess of love, but a deceptively pleasing-to-look-at power capable of reducing us to the level of fools. This fact is nicely depicted on a gem talisman from the Graeco-Roman period. The description of the talisman is contained in the following spell:

> Take a magnetic stone . . . design on it Aphrodite riding Psyche as on horseback, holding her with the left hand and doing up the locks of her hair. Below Aphrodite, and Psyche, Eros, standing upright on a globe: he holds a lighted torch with which he burns Psyche . . . on the other side of the stone, Eros and Psyche embracing.

On another gem, Syrian in origin, we find the same scene, the obverse side depicting the two lovers kissing above the inscription
"Curable love-wound."[27]

The figure of Psyche, a mortal maiden who first appears in the
tale of Amor and Psyche, refers us to what we now call the human
psyche. On this talisman she is depicted under the dominion of
Aphrodite, reduced to the state of an animal, a beast of the burden
of Aphroditic love. In short, the soul is represented in the service
of the instinctual and compulsive side of loving, for Aphrodite is
the goddess who inspires love of her, not of another. The intensity
of the service and submission is symbolized by the burning torch
of Eros, which on the coin is placed directly beneath Psyche's genitals. In other words, the purely erotic and instinctual ground of
being rides the soul, bareback, while gazing into a mirror. The
psyche is here at the beck and call of Aphroditic love with every
pull of the instinctual reins. One is inflamed by the burning torch
of Eros, and driven by Aphroditic self-involvement.

I am indebted to Prof. Donald Sheehan for telling me that the
tale of *Amor and Psyche* was the last to be created by the Classical
world before its downfall. This to me implies that the final message of the Classical world had to do with the nature of the soul
and the phenomenon of loving. In that the obverse side of the coin
mentioned above shows Eros and Psyche in close embrace, with
the motto, "Curable love-wound," it is implied that this compulsive quality of Aphrodite is a necessary road. And it is a road
that we today in our psychologies and counselling tend to advise
people against, for it smacks of pathology. Yet, the figure of
Aphrodite, if taken as an archetypal reality, informs us that she is
on the side of the nature of loving: the drive element of the divine
beast.

It is unsightly, ungainly, perhaps even a little frightening to
some of us — but who amongst us have not experienced if not in
reality, at least in phantasy, this seemingly unconscious and un-
civilized call to be ridden, driven, and burned by love? If Saturn in
the tale had seen what was contained in the compulsion of his
father, this experience would have been spiritualized to the point
that it is today in the East. There we find the figures of the divine
in ecstatic copulation, suggesting that what is sexual in us is divine.
And so it is to a point. But this particular attribute of making
divine what is mortal, devalues the mortal. What is mortal, basic,

and perhaps bestial, comes to be unacceptable unless it can be uplifted by a God-concept. When we view the sexual figures of the Orient, we allow ourselves the aesthetic privilege of finding what is pornographic in the West to be divine in the East. This is Kronos spiritualizing again. The inability to accept what is basic and base in humanity leads to a false aesthetics. Thus, the reason we have such a thing as pornography in the West — the graphic description of what Aphrodite is capable of demanding of us — is because Kronos did not see what was hidden in his father's compulsion. And it is just as well, for the issue of pornography is that it shows us realities we would rather deny on the one hand, while also revealing the extent to which humanity is capable of going with itself.

Now we must ask ourselves what is the difference between the compulsion of Uranos and that which is born of his genitals. At first sight they are the same, but the initial compulsion is materialistic in that it involves itself only with self-gratification, penetration of the world for one's own ends. Nothing comes of this other than power over the world. The compulsion of Uranos leads to a love of the concrete, accumulation of wealth, a filling up with possessions. Aphrodite on the other hand, can lead us beyond ourselves, to the other, and through the other reduce us, teach us that we alone are not the power. Her message is that the power resides in and through us, sometimes attacking through our genitals — for Aphrodite in classical times was the Goddess, obviously, of the genitals. More important, whereas in the first instance we may be reduced to her pack animal, if we are capable of enduring the trials that she imposes on the soul, we eventually gain union with Eros — with the loving void of compulsion. Kronos would keep us from that if he could. There are obviously instances when an individual in his or her chart displays a Kronian limitation in a variety of life situations. What then? Should one try to help them get past, around, or through the difficulty? Should one say, this is good for obviously you needed to be limited in this part of your life? Or should one instead say, go with the limitation to its fullest? Don't fight against it. It is what you are: see where *what you are* takes you.

I would choose the latter course, for to struggle against what you are is never to know fully what or who you are. The limitation of Kronos is a dark difficulty not to be got rid of by finding in it the gift of consciousness and courage, but rather by trusting that in your particular prison you will find what in you is separate and particular, what in you is individual and defining, what in you is explicitly yours, not to be shared with any other. To turn the darkness of Kronos into a "good" thing is to never experience the full nature of an archetype that suggests the dark night of the soul is the beginning of wholeness at the imaginal level. It is for this reason that Meister Eckhart wrote of Saturn as the dark purger who "in the heaven of the soul . . . becomes of angelic purity, bringing as reward the vision of God,"[28] and an alchemist wrote that "as lead burns up and resolves all the imperfections of the metals . . . so likewise tribulations in this life cleanse us from the many blemishes which we have incurred: wherefore St. Ambrose called it the key of heaven."[29]

But what of the loss of the Kronian rule in the tale of Hesiod? How does this come about and what is its meaning? As we mentioned earlier, Zeus caused Metis (insight) to administer an emetic to the God. Again, we find a water creature in a crucial role: Metis was the daughter of Oceanus — and obviously an aspect of soul according to the definition of Heraclitus. Zeus was later to swallow Metis, and thus for all eternity be capable of thinking and speaking with insight and wise counsel. In that Saturn contained all of the children who delineate the power and controlling aspects of consciousness, he can be thought of as a type of consciousness that operates from a power base, full of great ideas that he himself cannot put into action: again, the wise old man, the guru of the psychoanalytic couch, the ashram, and the astrological consulted hour. What releases the children of Kronos from their predicament is insight into Kronos. Insight makes the limiting and limited flow — which is exactly what happens to Kronos at this stage in the tale. There is a particular stage in the development of consciousness that demands we relinquish power, that we stop spiritualizing and lose the battle. Insight brings us to this point, and she brings it to us in a way that forces us to throw up and throw over all that we have assimilated of the world and of ourselves. It is at this point, at our weakest, no longer nourished by what we have carefully made and contained, that we fall as Kronos. There is a limit to consciousness itself, specifically Kronian consciousness, and at this moment we fall into ourselves.

Hesiod tells us that Kronos is banished to Tartaros, and he describes this as a region bounded by a bronze fence, backed up by a triple density of night or darkness, and surrounded by a wall. Here, he adds, we find the sources and ends of both the earth and the starry heaven. Atlas stands there holding the world upon his shoulders. Tartaros, in other words, is the beginning and end of *all* things. If Tartaros were destroyed, so too would the earth and starry heaven be. The support of all that we are, the heroic Atlas, would disappear. Obviously, Tartaros — this final prison of Saturn — is a special place. It is basic to human existence.

We are also informed that both day and night spend their time there, one at a time, greeting each other as they pass over the threshhold. The stay-at-home is obligated to hold in his or her arms the brother of death, sleep. Here, then, all opposites exist and find their root and resting place. Saturn is essentially the prisoner and lord of this place. Before this prison, Hesiod continues, are to be found the halls of Hades, Master of Souls. James Hillman has emphasized the fact that the underworld is the place of soul, and that access to soul can be gained only through an experience of death at the psychological level. The importance of such death reflects mythologically from the fact that in the regions of Tartaros /Hades our soul is stable, for as Plato points out: "The souls in Hades can neither be changed nor cured of what they are."[30] These regions are the only place where I can experience soul without fluctuations brought about by the intervention of consciousness.

The movement of Kronos from the upperworld to the underworld is a movement away from the realm of conscious-making, in the direction of soul-making. To follow Kronos here is to arrive at the base of my soul. This journey can be achieved only by insighting, by an archetypal imagining that allows the unconscious easy access to consciousness. It is a way of seeing, of visioning, that our culture describes as pathological — but which we find so attractive in Eastern cultures.

The horoscope of the individual is still a way for this vision to be achieved *if* the counsellor realizes that everything in a chart need not be interpreted but rather can be experienced and imagined. This is Jung's one true way in which we can transform nature — through the experience of the image first hand. This is also what Heraclitus meant when he wrote that "those who sleep are workers and share in the activities going on in the universe,"[31] for those who sleep are nightly engaged with the images given us by the deep psyche, sent up from the realm of Kronos and Hades.

Let me conclude by saying that the danger of Kronos lies in his lending us the illusion of age-old wisdom, while at the same time imprisoning us in a wisdom that is dry and cannot see outside of itself. The beauty of Kronos, on the other hand, is that he is a God who through tribulation is capable of bringing us to a full appreciation of ourselves from the pit of the soul.

The greatest danger for astrology is to be found in the Kronian tendency to spiritualize the person — to make of his chart a thing without soul. It would be a great pity if astrology were to become just another psychology of consciousness, for it is only in astrology where we find the Classical representations of the Gods and of the soul unabashedly presented as powers residing beyond the control of ego, as mysteries whose movements and effects might be clocked and predicted, but whose ulterior motives may never be understood. To lose this sense of mystery in favor of respectable acceptance would be the final insult the modern person could offer to the archetypal ground that daily effects us. Within the context of all that has been said above, it would be the curse of Saturn accomplished.

NOTES

[1]Jung, C.G., *The Collected Works* (CW), vol. 8, par. 964, Pantheon Books, New York, 1960.

[2]Corbin, Henry, "*Mundus Imaginalis* or the Imaginary and the Imaginal," *Spring: An Annual of Archetypal Psychology and Jungian Thought*, Spring Publications, New York, 1972, p. 11.

[3]Hillman, James, "The Dream and the Underworld," *Eranos Jahrbuch 1973*, E.J. Brill, Leiden, 1975, p. 256.

[4]Jung, CW 9, i, par. 50.

[5]For further information, see my *The Game of Wizards: Psyche, Science, and Symbolism in the Occult*, Penguin Books, Baltimore, Maryland, 1975, pp. 19-74.

[6]Freud, Sigmund, "A Child is Being Beaten," in *Collected Papers*, Basic Books, New York, 1959, vol. 2, pp. 197-8.

[7]Neumann, Erich, *The Origins and History of Consciousness*, Pantheon Books, New York, 1964, p. 125.

[8]Jung, C.G., CW 14, par. 222.

[9]*ibid.*, par. 223.

[10]*ibid.*, par. 223.

[11]Stein, Murray, "The Devouring Father," in *Fathers and Mothers*, Patricia Berry, editor, Spring Publications, New York, 1973, pp. 64-74.

[12]Paracelsus, *The Hermetic and Alchemical Writings of*, Shambhala, Berkeley, 1976, vol. II, p. 285.

[13]*ibid.*, p. 309.

[14]Paracelsus, *The Secrets of Alchymy*, R. Turner, trans., London, 1656, p. 21.

[15]Jung, CW 18, par. 149ff.

[16]Hillman, James, *Re-Visioning Psychology*, Harper & Row, New York, 1975, p. x.

[17]Jung, C.G., *Two Essays on Analytical Psychology*, Meridian Books, New York, 1956, p. 225.

[18]*ibid.*, p. 227.

[19]Jung, C.G., CW 8, par. 408.

[20]Hillman, James, "An Essay on Pan," *Pan and the Nightmare, Two Essays*, Spring Publications, New York, 1972, p. xxiv.

[21]Casey, Edward S., "Toward an Archetypal Imagination," Spring Publications, New York, 1974, pp. 1-32.

[22]Jung, C.G., CW 8, par. 189.

[23]Scott, Walter, ed. and trans., *Corpus Hermeticum*, Clarendon Press, Oxford, England, vol. I, p. 221.

[24]Wilhelm, Richard & Jung, C.G., *The Secret of the Golden Flower*, Wehman Bros., New York, 1955, p. 112.

[25]Freeman, Kathleen, *The Pre-Socratic Philosophers*, Harvard University Press, Cambridge, 1966, Heraclitus fragment 77.

[26]*ibid.*, frag. 36.

[27]quoted in Lindsay, Jack, *The Origins of Alchemy in Graeco-Roman Egypt*, Barnes & Noble, Inc., New York, 1970, p. 119.

[28]quoted in Jung, C.G., CW 14, p. 335, footnote 288.

[29]*ibid.*

[30]Plato, *The Collected Dialogues of*, Hamilton & Cairns, editors, Princeton University Press, Princeton, N.J., 1973, "Gorgias," 525e.

[31]Freeman, Kathleen, *op. cit.*, frag. 75.

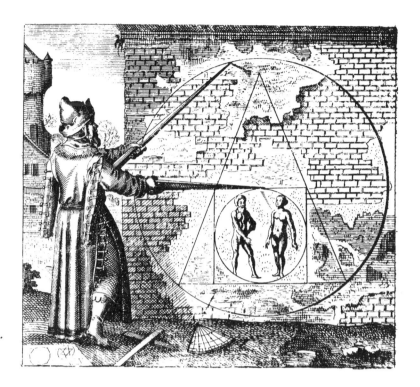

AN ALCHEMICAL ALLEGORY:
Notes Toward An Understanding Of Genesis

The OED informs us that 'archaic' defines that which is "marked by the characteristics of an earlier period: old-fashioned, primitive, antiquated." One would at first be reluctant to identify oneself with anything so defined. After all, the call of the Western psyche is that of the modern, the progressive, and the futuristic. The OED also informs us that 'modern' has its roots in the Latin *modo*, 'just now' or 'of today.' Yet, it is a rare event to find a 'just now' or 'of today' with the freshness of an isolated, independent, newly created moment. 'Just nows' are more often than not experienced as the flower of the 'just before,' of the archaic, of the antiquated. When I look at others, and in society in general, I cannot help recognizing that the attitudes and lifestyles, the philosophies and political systems that affect all of us fail to meet the definition of the modern. They may appear to define my 'just now,' my 'of the moment,' but the underbelly of their appearance is archaic. When I think of democracy, I think of the Greeks; of medicine, the Arabs; astronomy, the Babylonians; computers, Leibniz and the *I Ching*; Ethics, Aristotle; and Love, Socrates. I live by virtue of the Past.

When I turn to my own soul, I find that it fits the dictionary definition of the archaic. It is then that I am truly faced with the problem of the modern, of the 'just now.' If I am the expression of the soul, if all that I am is ultimately predicated by the dynamism of this deep interior principle, where am I to find my modernity?

This flow of soul is the constant of Being, and becomes the defining property of *bios* as long as I fail to separate the two and reconnect soul with the image of *zoe*, unlimited life. *Bios* defines an eternal ground. What my liver does today, it did seven thousand years ago, and could do seven thousand years from now. As long as soul is not differentiated from *bios*, there is no 'just now' or 'of today.' What makes a thing modern is the thing's relationship to the principle of unlimited life, for only the perception of *zoe* as the wings of soul can liberate the mind and the individual from the uninterrupted flow of the past back into itself. The perception of soul as *zoe* then leads to the future. The 'just now' can come about only by a purposeful intervention, an interruption of a psychological or spiritual nature that frees soul from the known and the expected so that it might lead us deeper into what is not fated in ourselves.

What is it that is not fated? The ground of our imagination which in the past was itself the method of transformation. Thus it was that Heraclitus, pointing towards the power of the image to connect us with the unlimited, wrote "Those who sleep are workers and share in the activities going on in the universe."

The way of transformation, the creation of the now, is image and imagination. And here is the paradox: what is modern in me can become so only by virtue of my conscious involvement with the archaic — with the soul. Such an involvement must take place at several levels, however. It is not sufficient that I work on myself and nothing more. I must also work on the image and myths that have worked on me through my culture. In that way, through that kind of work, we can all hope to liberate ourselves from cultural ideas; otherwise we are imprisoned by the endless passage through one imagination to another. As Ibn 'Arabi put it, "The whole of existence is imagination within imagination, while the true being is God alone."

It is with such considerations in mind that I offer the following, a preliminary attempt to understand a myth central to the psychology of our cultural background. Some of the proposals set forth may appear blasphemous, but to me the greater blasphemy is the silence that has surrounded the questions that the myth poses.

Hermaphrodism and the Fruit of Sin

The tale of *Genesis* is too well known to be repeated in its entirety. The important features necessary for our discussion are as follows:

1. God creates Adam in His own image.
2. He forbids him to eat of the Tree of the Knowledge of Good and Evil lest he die.
3. He creates Eve from a rib in Adam's side.
4. The serpent induces Eve to eat of the Tree and convince Adam that he should also.
5. Immediately upon eating of the Tree both their eyes are opened and they perceive each other's nakedness.
6. God discovers the 'sin' and banishes the two to the desert outside of Paradise.

There are many who will insist that this is a superficial outline of a tale replete with hidden meanings, and they would be right. But none of those meanings are on the surface of the tale. It is precisely because the surface of the tale has influenced our culture that we shall ignore these imagined subtler meanings. It is sometimes necessary when discussing such material to suffer the embarrassment of naked exposition, remembering all the while that it is a natural tendency to look for the hidden while overlooking the obvious.

The first symbol to be considered is that of the hermaphroditic Adam. The hermaphrodite, in general, must be recognized as a symbolic expression of two different types of psychic orientation or consciousness, the masculine portion representing all that may be identified with the male, the feminine with all that which may be identified with the female. And here we are faced with a problem, for each culture imposes certain of its own deficiencies and expectations into the definitions of these polarities. An apparent instance of this may be found in the general attitude that the feminine is the more inferior and weaker of the two; a less apparent instance, coming from contemporary quarters where the value of the feminine is undergoing rejuvenation, is that the masculine is self-centered and tyrannical. We must in our inquiry temporarily put aside any discussion of what may or may not be the true "qualities" of the masculine and the feminine and instead address ourselves solely to the fact of their polarity. It is not our place here to discuss sexuality *per se*, but rather to discuss the symbolism of the hermaphrodite which is basically asexual.

The figure of a bi-sexual being has been traditionally employed in the language of symbolism to demarcate the beginning and end of a process. To us in the West the most familiar figure of a beginning state is the original Adam containing his wife within him. The Jewish branch of mysticism known as Kabbalism recognizes the implications of this symbolism and traditionally has taken it also to symbolize the end of their mystical quest. To their way of thinking every man is both masculine and feminine. The Sefirothic system as paradigmatic of the human body is an apt depiction of this idea. The Christian European alchemist was in basic agreement with this Kabbalistic view, with the difference that the androgynous figure standing at the end of their process was the Christ in the form of the Philosopher's Stone. What is curious is that both Judaism and Christianity begin with and accept the figure of the hermaphrodite as well but neither of them hold the figure up as symbolic of a religious life. In each instance it was necessary that the renegade factor, the mystics and philosophers working outside of the mainstream of traditional religious belief, reveal the nature of the end process in these terms. The difference between the first and second representations of the bi-sexual being represents a unity that has come about through the agency of a transformative experience— one that has caused the polarities therein to perceive one another, suffer each other's differences, and reconcile their divergent natures under the auspices of love.

The opposites in their original hermaphrodite symbolize a condition of unconsciousness wherein they reside in blissful ignorance of one another. This original status also occurs, or is implied in those world mythologies where we are told that the anthropomorphic figures of heaven and earth as father and mother existed in an undivided state; so too in mystical theologies where the polarities expressive of the human condition are illustrated as entwined or enmeshed with one another: the Kundalini entwined around the lingam in Tantric yoga and the yin and yang as exemplary of two modes of action enmeshed in the figure of the T'ai Chi of Chinese philosophy. In each instance, the implication is that the figure is either symbolic of the androgynous total unity of God, or God himself.

When the God of *Genesis* "and all the host of heaven standing beside him on his right hand and on his left" (I *Kings* 22:19) said "Let us make man in our image, after our likeness" (*Genesis* 1:26), He too created a hermaphroditic figure modeled after Himself. However, the admonition given this newborn creature not to eat of the Tree of the Knowledge of Good and Evil implies that he is not a true image. At the most, the creature's awareness is limited to a process of naming (". . . and whatever the man called every living creature, that was its name" *Genesis* 2:19) similar to that encountered in a young child.

The radical alteration of God's image by His own hand that occurs when He extracts Eve from the body of Adam represents the first act of differentiation that occurs within the infantile psyche. Here, the first step away from the unconscious hermaphrodite is taken with the appearance of two distinct units or opposites. But with this first act of differentiation a strange event occurs. The division of the figures yields a type of creature God had not anticipated. Here for the first time the *possibility* of human consciousness occurs. And that possibility comes to fruition when Eve is induced by the Serpent to eat of the Tree and then to convince Adam to follow suit.

> Then the eyes of both were opened, and they knew that they were naked, and they sewed fig leaves together and made themselves aprons. (*Genesis* 3:7)

Suddenly, for the first time since their separation out of the original hermaphrodite modelled after their Maker the two *perceive* one another. They look at each other and see each other in their nakedness; they have feeling for one another. They have become Gods in that they are capable of perceiving the opposites, and it is this ability that abruptly separates them from the lower order of creatures, that makes them not only unique, but in part divine. For the divinity of being is consciousness, and consciousness is the one sin that we all commit when we move away from the commandments of the paradisical lassitude of our unconscious natures. It is for this first act of disobedience against the thing which would keep us as children, blind to the reality that everywhere touches us, that the gates of Paradise become barred. So too in the maturing child does there come a time when the free-floating pleasures of childhood suddenly end, the young ego seemingly cast out forever into the harsh and seemingly unsupportive desert of consciousness.

But one should not read too much into the idea that consciousness is in itself divine. It is that which makes us unique in the biological order because it has allowed us to create a second Genesis, the person-made world that overlays the world of nature. In this sense it is a miraculous happening, because of all forms of consciousness on the planet it is capable of concretizing the images that from time to time arise within us into created forms. So one might easily mistake the creative ability of human consciousness as divine, turning the diminutive ego into a hubristic monarch. What is divine in human consciousness, *per se*, is its ability to engage in soul-making activity as well as world-making. As James Hillman puts it, "The human adventure is wandering through the vale of the world for the sake of making soul. Our life is psychological, and the purpose of life is to make psyche of it, to find connections between life and soul."[1] For this we, both as men and women, need the Eve in us.

The harshness of the young ego's first encounter with all that exists outside of the paradisical unconscious is nowhere better illustrated than in the Apocryphal *Book of Adam and Eve* where we are told of Adam's several attempts at suicide immediately upon being cast out of Eden. Adam's predicament is a simple one: he is suddenly subject to the hardships of being-in-the-world, witness to the burden of consciousness that the ego must take up to accomplish successfully the transition from the paradise of a childhood free of conflict to the reality of the opposites of which our world appears to be composed. It is this willingness to take upon oneself the conflict of the opposites that exist beyond the gates of Paradise that gives birth to the transformative experience of suffering; it is this painful paradox to which the serpent awakens the first couple.

What we might have in the figure of Adam is a picture of the germinal ego coming into being in the pleroma of the unconscious.

That the Adam of Paradise represents what will become an important aspect of ego is implied in the fact that he is made in the image of God, and that as God rules over the paradise of the unconscious, Adam too will one day rule over the desert of consciousness existing beyond the Gates of Paradise. In short, the ego that rules consciousness is but the image of God, or the Self, that rules our unconscious.[2] The differentiation of this ego begins while it is still within the gates of the unconscious and is symbolized by the extraction of the feminine principle which (we are told) is of the essence of bone. That is, the feminine on the way to becoming has its origin in a thing many religions symbolically identify as eternal and divine. Even in our culture the skeleton, which alone remains after death, is symbolic of the barrier between the transpersonal and the mundane, between being and non-being. Both primitive and more advanced cultures employ different portions of the skeleton as *mana* objects, treating them as they would divinity itself. In addition, this feminine figure is taken from that portion of Adam's body closest to the heart — the place traditionally identified with emotion and intuitive knowledge. Eve is a portion of what is at once hidden but supportive, eternal and divine, wisdom-inducing and passionate; she symbolizes a component of our being that is both immortal and human; that mediates between being and non-being: the soul.

Universally it is the soul's function to mediate between the human world and the divine; she is often described as the bearer of messages in the form of dreams and visions — in other words, she operates through the realm of images. It is in this sense that the soul might be thought of as that which mediates between consciousness and the unconscious. It is because of the inquisitiveness of this soul principle that consciousness is won from the unconscious, that it is Eve who leads Adam to the fruit of the Tree. This too, traditionally, is a function of the soul: to inform, to direct, to guide, and to cause enlightenment. With this act of defiance the true separation from the unconscious takes place. The ego becomes locked out of Paradise, the soul going with it into the desert, her connectedness to the divine serving as the only link between the transpersonal and the mundane. The idea of the feminine soul exiled from the divine and trapped on earth is also a common theme in mythology and world religion.

Between the initial state of the hermaphrodite symbolic of the

unconscious union of the opposites and the final state of the androgyne symbolic of the marriage of all opposites in consciousness, there then appear the stages of life comprised of the conflict
of the opposites.

The Wisdom of the Serpent

"Now the serpent was more subtle than any other wild creature
that the Lord God had made." (*Genesis* 3:25). That the serpent is
"more subtle" is a major understatement. Here was the sole non-
human creature in the Garden not only capable of speech, but of
also knowing that God was lying to Adam when He told him that
the fruit of the tree would cause death. The serpent tells Eve she
need not fear the tree:

> You will not die. For God knows that when you eat of it your
> eyes will be opened and you will be like God, knowing Good
> and Evil.

The serpent is a cold-blooded creature who in at least one
system of transformation (Kundalini yoga) has been identified
with the sympathetic nervous system; that is, with the so-called
autonomous portion of our being. Because the serpent symbolizes
transformation through its activity of skin-shedding, and because
it knows the true results when the fruit of the Tree of Knowledge
of Good and Evil is eaten, we must assume that it represents yet
another form of consciousness. Considering the serpent and his relation to the first couple, it obviously represents the consciousness
of the psychic system that comes into being when the human
organism becomes a reality. It is, in other words, the inborn instinctual wisdom that God had not reckoned on, the spirit in
nature that complements the spirit of God hovering above the
waters of Creation. In the same manner that God is complemented
by the figure of Adam, so is the spirit of God complemented by the
spirit in nature. This is the core of our uniqueness. We contain a
spirit that is diametrically opposed to the Spirit of God who originally desired the perfection and stability of a Paradise. The spirit
of nature, on the other hand, demands imperfection and change,
for without these two states the need for and experience of transformation does not occur. This is something that God Himself had
no knowledge of originally: transformation. He was complete in

Himself, without imperfection. The serpent in psychological terms may be thought of as the cold-blooded range of instincts through which we experience transformation. Thus transformation comes to us through the instinctual range of our experience, through the first-hand experience of our autonomous nature.

All of which leads us to an important question: What is the serpent in relation to God? How is it that of all the creatures in the Garden it alone was capable of knowing God's most secret thoughts; what is it about this creature that allows it to know the true secret of the Tree, that allows it to know what even God Himself appears to be ignorant of — that the creature/Eve carries within her the seed of consciousness in the form of curiosity and that questions about the unknown are a temptation to her? Here we are obviously faced with a consciousness equal to God's in that it not only knows the past, the true value of the Tree, the psychic disposition of Eve, but also has some inkling of the potentialities inherent in the entire situation. We can only conclude from these facts that the serpent is symbolic of an aspect of God Himself, that its almost God-like consciousness is just that — a split-off portion of God's psyche.

The Dream of God

Now we must consider the phenomenon of Genesis from God's viewpoint, investigating the possible reasons for His committing Himself to the act. Throughout *Genesis*, up to the creation of the androgynous Adam, God goes about the entire matter of Creation in a rather straight-forward manner. We gain little insight into His psychology or His feelings until the day when He says to Himself:

> It is not good that the man should be alone; I will make him a helper fit for him. (*Genesis* 2:18)

In this statement we have a clue to why the project of Creation was ever undertaken, for God's ability to empathize with another's loneliness could only have grown out of a first-hand experience. There are a number of world mythologies that tell us the Creation of the universe arose from the Creator's experience of loneliness and the ensuing desire to create something that he could relate to. A vintage example is given us in the Winnebago Creation myth.

What it was our father lay on when he came to consciousness we
do not know. . . . He began to think of what he should do and
finally began to cry. . . . He said, "As things are just as I wish
them I shall make one being like myself." So he took a piece of
earth and made it like himself. Then he talked to what he had
created but it did not answer. He looked upon it and he saw that
it had no mind or thought. So he made a mind for it. Again he
talked to it, but it did not answer. . . So he looked upon it again
and saw that it had no soul. So he made it a soul. He talked to it
again and it very nearly said something. But it did not make itself intelligible. So Earthmaker breathed into its mouth and
talked to it and it answered.[3]

Again, in the *Satapatha Brahmana* we are told that the soul of
the universe, Purusha, was alone. Hence,

He did not enjoy happiness. He desired a second. He caused this
same self to fall asunder into two parts. Thence there arose a
husband and wife. From them men were born.[4]

The striking similarity between the Winnebago tale and
Genesis, right down to the creation of an Eve-soul for the creature
and the imparting of breath by Earthmaker to animate his creature
is apparent. Our example from Hindu mythology also
complements *Genesis* in that the Creator himself is a hermaphroditic creature whose division gives birth to the first couple. In
Genesis, God does not perform this operation on Himself but instead creates a creature in His own image in much the same
manner that the Winnebago God does. In both instances, as in
others too long to relate here, the creation begins because of God's
experience of loneliness. In our Western tale, God does not start
straight off with the creation of a divine couple but, as earlier in
the Winnebago tale, sets about the creation of the world proper.
The experience of loneliness, these tales appear to be telling us, can
be a creative experience if handled properly. That is, the experience if turned inwards unites one with unknown aspects of one's
own personality — in this instance, one's creative abilities. Ultimately, loneliness is something or someone representative or symbolic of an interior component of ourselves that longs to be united
with us, or that we long to be united with. Expressed psychologically, this yearning is for something that is not known to us consciously, that is hidden deep within our souls. We humans are afforded opportunities to gain access to the hidden portions of our-

selves through the agency of images that appear in either dreams, visions, or through methods that call forth the imaginative faculty of the unconscious. The latter constitute disciplined meditational techniques or a type of play that allows the unconscious to display itself during the waking state. Jung called this particular method (active imagination) a short-cut to the unconscious, for it allows inner being immediate access to consciousness, and *vice versa.*

Because in these versions the act of Creation grows out of a conscious decision on the part of God ("Let us make . . ."), we would here suggest that the Creation took place through an experiment in imagination. In an attempt to discover the hidden aspect of Himself with which He wished to be united, God allowed His unconscious to create an image of the material attempting to come into the light of consciousness. In much the same manner that the unconscious in human beings creates dreams reflective of our hidden nature, so too did God spin out of His unconscious that aspect of His hidden nature with which He was not reconciled. Whereas our unconscious lives are ephemeral and without material substance, His unconscious life took on substance. His images were to have as much life as the images we find in our dreams; His images were to live themselves forward regardless of His commandments in much the same manner that the process of our unconscious lives live themselves forward regardless of our conscious and rational commands. The creation of a creature in His own image constituted an attempt at introspection, an attempt to "get a look" at Himself, as it were. The androgynous Adam would therefore be symbolic of the unknown and hidden value that was attempting to become united with His consciousness. In other words, Adam symbolized the proverbial fly in the ointment, the unknown portion of God's psyche that constituted His blind spot.

The figure of Adam symbolizes the problem concealed in God's psyche; humanity represents the psychological process that God undergoes by committing Himself to an act of creative imagination. The pain and conflict that we undergo in our attempts at selfawareness are but symbolic of the same process God undergoes through the history of the human race. We are the conflict, the pain, the confusion of His own transformation. History is God's self-analysis. We are His dream over which He has as little control as we do ours. For us to affect the nature of our dream lives creatively and positively we must first arrive at a proper conscious standpoint in our relationship with the unconscious. So too, we assume, must God act toward his "unconscious," the sphere of which is the created world, if He is to realize the dark and unknown aspect of his own personality symbolized by the serpent. This now brings us to the question of what God might have been unconscious of to begin with.

The Serpent on the Cross

The experience of loneliness, the yearning for the unknown and unseen within us, the thing scratching at our dreams, can, if not properly attended to, lead us into states of inexplicable rage. Invariably, one ends up vacillating between the experience of extreme emotion and boredom. As Paul Tillich once surmised, boredom is rage spread thin. The phenomenon of rage presents us with a peculiar ambiguity. On the one hand, a person overcome with rage usually appears to be acting out of a passionate emotion, in the "heat of anger" as it is usually referred to. On the other hand the results of such a state are actually unfeeling acts. Hidden within this so-called heat of anger is a cold-blooded instinctual response to situations that the individual for some reason or other finds untenable. One aspect of the symbolism of the serpent in the tale of *Genesis* is just this type of cold-bloodedness. In the light of the frequent outbursts of rage that the *Old Testament* God often displays, we would suggest here that the serpent (which we have described as a split-off portion of God's psyche) symbolizes the cold-blooded and instinctual side of God's unrealized difficulty. The fact that God is not aware of the knowledge that the serpent contains, the fact that he overlooks its presence in the Garden of his imagination, indicates that He is not only blind to this rage, but that He has actually repressed it out of sight. In that the serpent is also symbolic of transformative powers and consciousness; the secret of God's problem is to be discovered in the very thing that He rejects. However, rage and cold-bloodedness, loneliness and boredom are only symptoms. The serpent is but the energic principle of the unrealized problem symbolized by the hermaphroditic Adam. The problem is to be found in God's unity.

What the image of Himself reveals to God is the fact that the unity He represents is composed of opposites. Because God, not only in our tradition but in every tradition known to us, is defined as a unity of opposites, the one thing that He cannot know of is the experience of the opposites in a divided state. God has the *knowledge* of the opposites, but not the *experience* of their effect. He has experienced only their peaceful unity. The knowledge that He has of them constitutes a philosophical assumption. In order to experience the true effect of the opposites He must first divide them. This is the nature of God's blind spot in *Genesis*, the source of his rage in the *Old Testament* — this little piece of unconsciousness concerning an aspect of His psyche of which He has had no experience.

So, the events of *Genesis*, from the beginning up to the expulsion from Eden, are symbolized throughout by division. With the division of the androgynous Adam into male and female the process of self-awareness begins. However, as is more often than not the case, this first attempt to take a look at Himself fails, for He assumes (as we also so often do) that He knows exactly what He looks like, knows without a doubt all the components of His personality. Adam, however, is a pure intellectual construction, for he is made up of those things that God chooses as relevant for his creation. The active and motivating principles of His problem, the energy necessary for transformation symbolized by the serpent, is repressed, overlooked, lurking in the Garden's shadows. Adam as symbolic of God's problem is an intellectualization similar to those lists we often compose as illustrative of our good and bad qualities. God does not really want to consider the moral problems posed by His knowledge of Good and Evil, hence He leaves those qualities out of the image He would employ as an introspective aid. But the unconscious will not allow Him to escape the issue. The repressed value intrudes itself and sets up a situation in which the moral issue He does not want to consider is presented to Him in a symbolic play. It shows Him that the repressed value contains transformative energies and a consciousness of its own; that to achieve consciousness and discover the nature of one's own inferiority it is at times necessary to go against one's own ego-dominated commandments. In this regard, the serpent symbolizes the innate wisdom of the instinctual portion of the psyche to heal and transform itself. It attempts to reveal this fact to God, but instead of pausing long enough to consider that the mishap came about because of an error in His judgement, He elects to pass the blame on. The suffering that would have arisen by His wrestling with the problems in the issue of Good and Evil is instead heaped on the shoulders of His creation. In other words, He represses the problem even further through projection.

What the serpent attempted to show God on the stage of Paradise was that transformation can be experienced only by a willingness to take on the suffering implicit in any act of becoming consciouss; that to gain access to an unrealized portion of His own being, God would have to experience the conflict of the opposites at first hand. To achieve this He would have to commit Himself totally to the experiment. The task would have been easier if He had dealt with it within the confines of His carefully constructed vessel called Paradise. Having failed in that experiment, He would have to follow the lead that the psyche imposed on Him. He would have to experience the conflict *in* the world, which in His reality meant that he would have to make a total descent into His unconscious. In short, He would have to become mortal in the figure of the Christ in order to experience the conflict peculiar to humanity. It would only be there, on the Cross, in that mass of nerve and muscle, that God could experience what was unknown to Him: the conflict inherent in the disunity that expresses itself in suffering. It was only in this manner that the symptoms of His unconsciousness could be transformed. It was there where the serpent of His psyche would in time be experienced firsthand by that manifestation of Himself in the form of the Christ who would himself say, during a discussion on the necessity of being reborn:

> And as Moses lifted up the serpent in the wilderness, so must the Son of man be lifted up, that whoever believes in him may have eternal life. (*John* 3:14,15)

And in such a manner was God eventually to resolve his psychic difficulty. From a wrathful, vengeful, and unpredictable despot He was transformed into a God of Love through the agency of our humanity. It is through this act of transformation that the androgyne appears in the person of Christ who by his traditional identification with the Second Adam becomes associated with the bi-sexual figure which began the process.

The Christ therefore symbolized the suffering inherent in the fusion of the divine with the human portions of our psyches. That is, it is at that point where we suffer the greatest anguish in the desert of this world to which we have been exiled that we may know we are contributing to the self-realization of God Himself. It is only during such moments in the Work that we may fully know we are in the presence of the archetypal.

And in all this there is concealed the meaning of the statement that the Stone is the Christ and that the stages of the Work are revealed to us in the seven days of Creation. By this it is to be understood that God's task was that of separating the opposites so that He could experience their differences: and that our task is that of uniting the opposites so that we might have the knowledge of their unity, which is God.

This is the meaning of the marriage of the sun and moon, of the solar and lunar consciousness we have been allotted, and without whose union we deny God the experience of Himself.

NOTES

[1]*Re-Visioning Psychology*, James Hillman, Harper & Row Publishers, New York, 1975, p. ix.

[2]*vide*, C.G. Jung, "The ego . . . is a relatively constant personification of the unconscious . . ." CW 14, p. 107.

[3]quoted in *From Primitives to Zen*, Mircea Eliade, Harper & Row, New York, 1967, pp. 83-4.

[4]*ibid.*, p. 151.

WOMAN, THE FEMININE,
AND ALCHEMY

In truth, what follows are considerations on the nature of man, specifically his unconscious condition as expressed in his religious and mystical experience. In all aspects of this experience we find a theory of woman which is at first sight romantic, but on closer inspection demeaning. I bring these issues up in the manner of a suggestion — that as we in the secular world now begin the business of re-defining the roles of men and women, we not lose sight of the fact that practically all of our mystical traditions are the creations of men and that in these systems there may lie concealed, in poetic garb, those same insinuations of masculine superiority that we now discover in the mundane sphere.

All of this would point to the idea that many aspects of our mystical and religious traditions must be reconsidered if they are

to be married to reality—and married they must be if we are to
ever become one with that which we call God.

I for one do not find it possible to speak *to* woman of either her
psychology or her present condition. At most, I may speak of my
relationship to the feminine, and from there the nature of my
awareness of Woman as an Other. And here is the crux of the
problem. Each of us, men and women alike, are contained units,
monads of pure energy or "windowless beings" as Leibniz put it.
Much in our relationships is based upon assumption and
phantasy. We came together in a seeming unity of understanding
based on shared experiences in which we find a similarity of response. Ultimately, all of our feelings towards one another are
based on an imaginal realm of hazy similitude, or at least the feeling of conviction that "we know" what the other is feeling, has felt,
is experiencing. The closer we are in terms of sex, background,
education, religion, etc., the less pronounced is the effect of this
imaginal realm. But when we are confronted with an Other, one
whose biological structure is different from ours, the imaginal
quality of the relationship becomes heightened and the vacuum of
our ignorance becomes a vessel for the imperceptible—for the
soul.

I do not mean to imply that the experience of those aspects of
soul that are felt as personal can only be known in love relationships between members of the opposite sex. I make reference to the
image of the couple as a team in this essay solely because it appears
often in alchemy, the implication being that the work is one concerned with the oppositional and distinctively different qualities of
certain psychic realities. At the same time, however, while the soul
can be experienced through a deep encounter with an idea, a condition, a work, it is doubtful that a real engagement can occur
without a considerable measure of loving.

The feeling of "knowing the Other," the intensity of the knowledge of the Other "body and soul" should not be set aside as mere
illusion, for it is the very thing that bonds humankind together.
This feeling of "knowing," the intimacy of a shared experience, is a
phenomenon of love or Eros. Because I speak here of Eros as a
Power, a dynamic energy of an archetypal nature, a God in the
classical sense, its intimacy should be understood as a total recept-
iveness to and common containment in the God Himself. This, essentially, is what being *in* love means.

The alchemists knew that this imperceptible quantity is the thing called forth in an encounter with an Other, with either the wife as "fellow worker," or the image of the female as counterpart. In either case, what we are talking about is the image of the soul and the idea that one's relationship with that image will always be a determining factor in any real encounter with others. This is all the more reason why it is imperative at this juncture in history to review the image of soul in alchemical, religious, and mythological thought. This must be done to determine whether the earlier views are commensurate with the insights of our twentieth-century experience or were from the outset generalizations founded on a basic misunderstanding of the nature of the opposites.

In the long run it is only through an acknowledgement of our interiority that we may come to see the Other as a person and not as a fragment of our imprisoned souls projected upon them. Without such an acknowledgement all forms of soul-work must be considered worthless.

> The union of the sexes is four-membered rather than two-membered: it always means the complex union of the male element of the one with the female element of the other, and of the female element of the first with the male element of the second. The mystical life of the androgyne is realized not in one bisexual being but rather in the quadripartite union of two beings. (Nicholas Berdyaev)

There appears to be a universal law, unfortunate in its implications, which states that wherever you find a religious or mystical system that exalts the feminine, making of it a divine attribute through which salvation may be known, in the society where that view is furthered you will find a proportionate disregard of woman as social being. One can almost postulate a law of compensation. From the Virgin Mary to Shakti to Yin and to the Shekhinah of Kabbalistic doctrine, the case holds true. Woman as a spiritual factor is the desired, but woman as an existent in her own right is exemplary of a downfallen clod of earth.

The first point in fact is the Kabbalistic doctrine that tells us that the feminine portion of God, the Shekhinah, is in exile in the world. In the configuration known as the Sefirothic Tree of Life we find a fourfold division known as the Four World system. The doctrine of this system will be known to most of my readers. For those who are not familiar with it let them know that I am here concerned only with the problems presented by the fourth world, that associated with this world, our earth.

In the Sefirothic system the fourth world is identified with the sefirah Malkuth, The Kingdom, which is again symbolic of our place of existence. This sefirah Malkuth *is* the Shekhinah, the ex-iled feminine portion of God that longs to be united with Him — and with good reason, for she represents the grossest part of creation in which reside the evil spirits known as the *kellipoth*.

To make matters worse, the triad of the Kabbalistic soul, which is also described as feminine, is thought of as manifesting it-self along the course of the first three worlds. That is, the first and purest portion of the soul is associated with the sefirah Kether, that sefirah furthest removed from mankind. The second portion of the soul, that which is synonymous with the moral element of God, is identified with the sefirah Tifereth which unites the Sef-iroth of the second world. Lastly, the third division of the soul, that portion which is identified with the animal life and desires and unites the Sefiroth of the third world, is located in the sefirah Yesod, the sefirah symbolic of the male and female genitals. The fourth world, however, that which *is* the feminine, the Shekhinah, God's helpmate and love, *has no share of the soul*. It is soulless.

Add to this the disconcerting fact that the salvation of man-kind, the restitution of the divine portion of God to God, was con-sidered by both the Rabbinic and Kabbalistic tradition to be the work and concern of men, a divine job in which woman as social being played no role other than that of model of the catastrophe known as the Fall, and you have a pretty good picture of the atti-tude towards woman in that mystical setting.

Turning to the Orient we find matters just as bad, with yin and yang representative of woman and man respectively. The yang is defined as that which is light and positive, the yin as that which is dark and negative. For a Taoist monk to achieve the balance of these opposites within himself, to equilibriate his over-plus of in-nate yang, he must acquire a proportionate amount of yin. This is accomplished through sexual intercourse with as many "holy" women as possible in succession without achieving ejaculation until the end of his adventure. When that moment finally does oc-cur the practitioner must perform "retention of seed," during which time it is imagined that the semen is channelled up through the spine, the end-result being the birth of the inner-man. No mention is ever made of the woman's development in this process outside of the fact that she is "honoured."

The social position of women in ancient China is too well-known to be discussed here, but the extent to which this mystical doctrine of the opposites was taken may be seen in the following quote from a work entitled *Nu-chieh* (*The Ideal Woman*):

> The sexual union depends on Yang's ability to dominate and guide, and Yin's willingness to follow and obey. Man is wonderful for his strength, woman for her simple submissiveness . . . In the bedchamber the woman must discourage excess by her restraint, not by opposing Yang, but by transforming her own wish for "fire inside the Jade Pavilion" (orgasm) into transcendental thoughts. Excess of *Clouds and Rain* (sexual intercourse) will lead to moral depravity and finally to use of lewd words. Such a state can only result in the calamity of wifely disrespect for her master . . . A woman must be chaste and respectful, choose her words carefully, never show distress, avoid laughter or jestful behavior, refrain from peeping from windows and mixing with crowds. If she is at all times as discrete as a shadow or an echo, who can find fault with such a woman?

A good example of the Hindu attitude is to be found in the Tantric text *Kama-Kala-Vilasa* where we find a myth of the Creation. There we are told that the Great Lord Shiva, discovering that he was alone in the universe, spun out of his loneliness Desire in the shape of the Divine Feminine, his Shakti. No sooner did she see and realize his beauty when there arose in her a desire for him to experience his magnificence. To this end she transformed herself into "The Pure Mirror in which Shiva experiences Himself." Again, in an attempt to express her awe and love for Him, Shakti then went on to create out of her own body the manifest worlds of substance and sensation, the lowest and grossest being our world with which she becomes identified. All of this is rather interesting when one considers that the yogin's goal is disengagement from the world in his union with a masculine God.

And then, finally, there is our own tale of Creation where woman is created not in her own right but as a smaller portion of man. In Hebrew the word for "a woman" is *ishshah*, which is defined as a *creature* having the general appearance of a man, differing only in sex. The selection of the name *Chavvah* (Eve) is also interesting in that the Hebrew *Chavvah* is curiously reminiscent of the word for "beast," *Chayyah*.

In all of the above examples we find the feminine associated with the damned earth which is in turn the harbor of evils and the prison of the feminine. In every instance it is implied that woman or the feminine is, if not of lesser origin, certainly of a lesser state of being. The only saving feature throughout is the implication that it is necessary that the feminine be re-united with the divine. There is an urgency to this idea. There is something within the soul that is infinitely wiser than the machinery of our intellects, something which knows that things have gone amiss and that a general state of restitution is imperative.

> And I find more bitter than death the woman, whose heart is snares and nets, and her hands as bands: who so pleaseth God shall escape from her; but the sinner shall be taken by her. (*Ecclesiastes* 7:26)

> Let the woman learn in silence with all subjection. But I suffer not a woman to teach nor to usurp authority over the man, but to be in silence. For Adam was first formed, then Eve. And Adam was not deceived, but the woman being deceived was in the transgression. Notwithstanding she shall be saved in childbearing, if they continue in faith and charity and holiness with sobriety. (*I Timothy* 2:11-15)

> And if they will learn anything, let them ask their husbands at home: for it is a shame for them to speak in church. (*I Corinthians* 14:35)

What all of these traditions point to is a deficiency, a hole in the pleroma of our being that has so long been ignored that now the soul announces the problem in the most secret of our palaces — our bedrooms and our sexual instincts. This deficiency has gone so long unnoticed, even though our myths and our religions are replete with insinuation of its existence, that it now attacks us directly in the form of sexual and psychological problems, in those breakdowns of spirit we term impotence and frigidity.

*   *   *

"You will never arrive at any perfection unless Sol and Luna be united into one body."
—Laurentius Ventura

*   *   *

In every instance, the feminine is described as that which is debased, uncomely, and weak. This then is the lot of our humanity: to suffer the rejected portion of our souls. Psychology would step in here and call those portions repressed, but they are more than repressed, for the term implies that they were once known to us and purposively cast out of our lives. Nothing could be further from the truth. The condition described in these texts is a given. Thus, what alone can lead me towards my own salvation is the very thing that most naturally repels me. The alchemists were aware of this state of affairs when they wrote that the true gold is to be found in the filth by the wayside, in that which has been discarded. As they used to say, it is all around us, before our eyes, in the world. It is the archetype of the feminine: Mother-nature, sister-soul, wife-companion. It is also the archetype of matter, of stuff that makes things real. That myths inform us the feminine is matter itself implies that everything that becomes *a* matter, everything that has or gives substance to our lives must be archetypally feminine. If there is any one definition of the feminine here, it is that the feminine as matter defines any situation in which an issue having to do with one's basic and simple existence comes to the fore. We might add that issues bearing strong emotional difficulties, of a type one would prefer to reject out of hand, by corresponding with the archetypal figure of the rejected feminine also define the most important aspect of the feminine.

Whatever I ultimately define as my world, the person-created value systems that hold together my way of being in the world, that give meaning and support to my life, there is where the feminine is. She is to be found in the particulars of a life, in the foundation of any temple I might create. She is the symptom of my being, the thing that connects me to reality in a most painful way, that turns me away from the heights of conscious fabrications towards the depths of what has been given me as myself. What the feminine suffers in myth is essentially what I suffer in the myth of myself, for the feminine is not some mythological abstract reality — it is a portion of myself that it tightly knit to life, if not life itself.

In all of the myths referred to the world of humanity comes into existence *because* of her exile, her fall, the losing of her way. My humanity, everything that I define as human, ultimately has its origin in the archetypal condition of the feminine so described. If she is orphaned, I am orphaned, and if she is lost then so too am I. Wherever I fall, become lost or exiled, there I am *in* soul. And if

she is also described as the body — which she is — then my most
intimate connection to her will be through my body. But, again, it
will be through all of these perceptions of body as base, not to be
discussed, hidden away from dining-room conversations. Where
my body breaks down, where my body demands of me what I
would not give it, where my body embarrasses or repels me, there
is the dark one of Solomon.

The depreciation of the feminine, and hence of women, since
the beginnings of the Classical Period, reveals the existence of an
archetype of inferiority. That is, there is in the psyche of mankind
and womankind an idea of something inferior, dark, weak, exiled
and soulless. This archetypal structure at some point in our development became projected out into the world on to women and
all which is defined as feminine. It points to the existence of a split
in our being that has been instrumental in the creation of institutions wherein the female and the feminine have been placed in a
subordinate position. If one moves backwards into the psyche to
discover the root of this attitude, what one finds is an attitude towards soul, towards the feminine aspect of the Divine. The exile of
the feminine in matter as imagined by the alchemists, the personification of the feminine as earth, was considered correctly by them
to signify the exile of Soul from its place in the world of being.

The fear of the feminine in the world and in ourselves is exemplary of our attitude towards that out of which it has arisen —
the sea of the unconscious which even when it was "discovered" by
Freud was thought of as nothing more than a garbage heap of re-
pressions. That the earth was at one and the same time a synonym
for the human body and for the feminine indicates that the alchemists understood that the problem was one of redeeming what
is "feminine" in ourselves.

                    *   *   *

When the period was completed, the bond by which all things
were held together was loosed, by God's design; all living
creatures, having till then been bisexual, were parted asunder,
and man with the rest; and so there came to be males on the one
part, and likewise females on the other part. (*The Poimandres of
Hermes Trismegistus*, Book I, 19)

                    *   *   *

Spirit is, with very few exceptions, not only thought of as masculine, but as volatile and uncontained, free-ranging. Soul, on the other hand, is invariably thought of as feminine, imprisoned contained, and dedicated to nothing but union with the masculine thought of in the singular sense. In other words, Spirit is an undiscriminating and free-wheeling potency, whereas Soul is a highly discriminating and limited potential.

Traditional mythologies point to this biased fact time and again, and should be thought of as attempts to show us our condition so that we might learn where the alchemical work is to be performed, where it is that we may come into contact with what we are. The dichotomy presented to us in these tales points not to what should be used to define our social and personal relationships, but rather what defines our initial relationship to ourselves — the so-called *natural* man or woman, if you would. The dichotomy points to the split within each of us, and the employment of sexual imagery to emphasize the differences and difficulties between these polarities is an attempt to show us that the differences are basic, natural, and in the end define our humanity. But the humanity they point to is not the anthropological, the sociological, or the statistical. It is *my* humanity; the male and female of me and in me, the Adam and Eve wandering through the world on a daily basis, seeking relief from what I am.

To derive from this the idea that we are in need of transformation is to evade the issue. Transformation implies a change from bad to better, a movement away from the difficult to the manageable or sublime. To seek transformation of the feminine is to deny its reality as an archetypal given. To say the feminine is in a state of damnation and filth that must become glorified and cleansed is to deny the feminine. And yet we have made a cult of transformation. Spiritual, religious, and psychological programs all demand that we transform ourselves. And the demands that these systems place upon us is one that would have us reject the basic nature of the feminine and soul. To become better, I must reject what I am for what I should be. Invariably, what I should be is also what everyone else should be as well. The call for transformation, therefore, especially in the twentieth century, is but a call to the common, to the equal, and to the acceptable. It is the religion of a spiritual democracy that assumes all parts of myself are equal in the eyes of God. But a nightly appraisal of myself alerts me to the fact that there is much in me that is not equal. My desires and my limitations are at variance with one another. And yet simply to demand that I reduce my desires to the tight fit of my limitations would be to take away the enthusiasms natural to life — to give in and give up.

The systems of transformation that travel in magical mystery show style from one part of this country to another all at some point or another inform us that to become whole we must struggle against being ourselves. There is something wrong with this attitude, for by refusing to accept the infirmities that define us, we also refuse the soul.

If not transformation, what then? Are we simply to be and nothing more? Are we simply to exist like the flowers and the birds? I think not. This too is yet another system of transformation: our mis-reading of the Taoist "not doing." The assumption behind such a call is that everything that is in or of Nature is good and all we need do is become one with Nature. But it is curious that what is murderous, bestial, sick, dying or dead in nature never enters into the picture of this spiritual program either. Only what is beautiful and without conflict is natural. So, this is no way of depth for us either.

Karl Kerenyi has alerted us to the idea that a symbol "is the visible sign of an invisible order . . . a transparent part of the world," to be seen through.[1] And he refers us to the world as the source of symbol, not the other way around. We generally tend to think of the symbol as something other than ourselves, above or beyond us. But what if situations and realities so commonplace as to be overlooked are themselves the symbols of what Kerenyi calls an invisible order. It is not the invisible order that is symbolic, it is the visible order. And this latter order is simply the surface of a happening that *is* of itself and nothing more. It has no meaning in the psychological or hermeneutic sense but is rather a statement of archetypal fact. If so, then I would have no right to take my broken arm as an omen that something should be transformed. My condition *has already been transformed.* What I am being called upon to do at that moment is to see through experience to the archetypal lineaments of that fact. James Hillman has defined this first stage in seeing through as "a process of interiorizing,"[2] and obviously what we need for it is another set of eyes to see what is not immediately transparent.

So it is not a matter of my transforming what I am or what has become of me as much as it is a matter of my immersion in what I am to the fullest. And if this should pain me, constrict me, bind me then that is the meaning for it aptly describes the mythological experience of the soul and is a way into my soul. The meaning is the experience of myself and nothing more—but I must also be constantly aware that the "myself" I speak of is but a symbol of an invisible order. What mythology describes as the feminine must be seen through. We must reconsider many so-called spiritual truths by virtue of the fact that they may have in many instances been restated, molded, and modified by the existing social *mores* at that time when they became manifest.

In the puberty rites of male-societies the initiate is forced to cut himself off from the feminine sharply and distinctively (from the mother in particular), by acts of heroism that demand he go against his instinctual nature. It is not so much that the initiate is asked to separate himself from his mother as much as it is that he is called upon to free himself from what she symbolizes—the maternal aspects of the instincts and the deep unconscious. When functioning normally, the instincts "take care" of us—tell us when we need food, when we should advance, when we should flee, fight, befriend, etc. I understand this maternal realm to symbolize the unconscious upon which the individual is initially dependent, moved by impulses rather than by decisive and willed actions.

During the time when we are cared for by the instinctual realm, during childhood, practically any response or activity is allowed us by society. When we leave the realm of the maternal, however, we are expected to work against nature. During a man's initiation, for instance, he is not allowed to retreat, flinch, or complain of the pain inflicted upon him in any manner. In all such initiations the initiate must remain still, receiving the most painful treatment without a word or sign of discomfort. In some societies such reactions bring instant death. What is demanded is that one become independent of the maternal realm of his own being, that one through decisive action overcome instinctual response.

In an Hungarian fairy tale called *The Glass Axe* we are told the story of a Queen who on her deathbed commands her husband to,

> Never let the child [her son] put his feet on the ground, for as soon as he does so he will fall into the power of a Wicked Fairy, who will do him much harm.

As the boy grows he is carried on litters, wheeled about in chairs, and finally given a horse which he must always ride. While hunting one day he falls from his horse and touches the ground at which time, "A whole new world stretched out before him." He is then given a task by the Wicked Fairy with the warning that should be encounter a black girl in the woods he is not to speak to her on pain of death. Of course, he meets the girl and does speak with her only to discover that she is the enchanted daughter of the Wicked Fairy. To make a long story short, she promises to aid him in his tasks, one of them being the murder of the Wicked Fairy herself. With the aid of the black girl the day is won and they are wed to live happily ever after.

In this tale we find the Prince protected by the queenly aspects of the feminine, those that are removed from the basics of everyday life, ensconced in the castle heights, maternal in its protection. Much of our present involvement in the idea of the feminine and the need to reconcile ourselves with it focuses on this queenly dimension. The modern adoration of the feminine is an adoration of the feminine removed from us. It is the spiritual but distant protector capable of caring for us even in death. Whether we call this type of femininity the anima, shakti, or the Virgin Mary we cannot escape the fact that she does not allow us to come into contact with the immediate ground of our world. If anything, she encourages us to be carried about in spiritual smugness. We write papers and give lectures on the beauty of the feminine, the conjunction with the feminine, the reconciliation with the masculine portion of our psyches with the feminine — all the while refusing to see that what we applaud is not soul, but Mother. We are protected at every turning by our phantasy of the feminine as something purely pleasant and complementary.

What is it that this Queen would protect us from? From the earth, the dirt of our commonality, the dark and damned connection to soul. And the tale tells us, quite simply, that in order to come into contact with this reality one must literally fall off of one's high horse. Only then does a new world open to us. The darkness of the exiled feminine approaches us so that we can truly marry. One need only refer to the Song of Solomon to discover the significance of the maiden who is "black but comely." And it is here that our comments in "Paracelsus and the Wound" regarding our disregard of the body particularly apply.

The contrast between fairytales featuring issues central to the male psyche and those concentrating on female issues is marked. In the latter, the woman is either possessed or in a state of imprisonment during the greater part of her experience. She is either asleep or entranced, transformed into a small helpless creature or dwelling in a class or position beneath her station. She is, as our brief survey of creation myths revealed, trapped, exiled, and helpless. In every instance her life is in danger and can be saved only through the agency of the masculine, and then only through love. But the most significant clue is that the masculine himself is also in a helpless state, as in the Polish fairytale *The Crow*.

There we are told of the youngest of three Princesses who one day comes upon a torn and bleeding black crow that claims he is an enchanted Prince. He tells her that if she wished, she could save him on the condition that she "say good-bye to all of your own people and come and be my constant companion in this ruined castle. There is one habitable room in it, in which there is a golden bed . . . You will have to live all by yourself . . . and whatever you may see or hear in the night you must not scream out, for if you give as much as a single cry my suffering will be doubled." To this the Princess agrees. After two years of horrifying experiences, through all of which she remains silent, the crow comes to her and adds,

> "Before I can resume my natural form . . . you must go out into the world and take service as a maidservant."

This accomplished, the Prince is transformed and they too live happily ever after.

There are countless other variations on this theme, the most familiar found in the tale of *Beauty and the Beast*. In every instance we come upon the following conditions:

1. She must leave her people.
2. She must be totally dependent upon herself during her time of trial.
3. She must suffer silently.
4. She must live with a possessed creature.

In every instance the woman must marry the male principle in its most unseemly form in order to aid it in its transformation. It is interesting to note that the male principle is invariably cast in the form of a beast or monster. The problem, these tales appear to be telling us, is that the feminine in freeing herself must accept the raw instinctual portion of herself.

As with the myths discussed earlier, these fairy tales on the one hand reveal the nature of the split between the masculine and feminine principles and the necessity of redeeming the lost value of the Other. Because the male in our society has been allowed publicly to live out his instinctual side without fear of ostracization, during which time he must repress only the feeling-side of his psyche — the stratum of tears, warmth, affection and aestheticism which have come to be identified as feminine — because he has been allowed expression of his instinctual realm, his problem in transformation has to do with the "killing" and therefore transforming of the beast in order to redeem the feminine.

The woman on the other hand is taught at an early age to suppress if not repress the instinctual side of her nature, the "beastial" portion of her psyche, the expression of which *would* lead to public ostracization. The tales reveal that her problem calls for an acceptance of the beast within.

Again, in the realm of fairytales this time, we are warned that we have repressed the other half of our being. True, the feminine in these tales does not take on the negative connotations that we found in our religious texts as an inherent condition. But the idea that the feminine must *purposively* take on the qualities and conditions which bespeak degradation appears to indicate the presence of a compensatory law of the psyche which has become perverted into a "true and natural" depiction of the feminine and therefore of woman in general. That is, whereas the fairytale presents us with temporary and purposively adapted modes of activity the fabricators of myths, mystical systems, and *mores* have mistakenly portrayed these modes as *natural and inborn distinctions*, inescapable and permanent features of what we are to understand as the definitive statement regarding the makeup of the masculine and the feminine.

In other words, we have taken the portrayals of the masculine and the feminine at the highpoint of a transformative act and frozen them in mid-air, leaving ourselves with the one-sided ideas of the masculine as aggressive and out-going, dressed in battle-garb, and the feminine as docile and introverted, dressed in the fabric of scullery maid and housekeeper.

The tale of the Prince tells us of the nature of polarities inherent in the feminine, whereas the tale of the Princess tells us of the soul's experience of itself. The mythological themes of the soul's exile are here repeated at the level of secular story-telling. But it is the same story. The injured beast is myself in need of soul's caring, and that caring places the soul in a different position. It is through my difficulties that I become reconciled with what is defined as basic in the feminine. What I see through sees through me, too. The Prince and the Princess are a new Adam and Eve, both caught in the myth of myself where the two tales occur at one and the same time.

      *   *   *

Then she began to bark also, crawling after him — barking in a fit of laughter, obscene and touching. The dog began to cry then, running with her, head-on with her head, as if to circumvent her; soft and slow his feet went padding. He ran this way and that, low down in his throat crying, and she grinning and crying with him; crying in shorter and shorter spaces, moving head to head until she gave up, lying out, her hands beside her, her face turned and weeping; and the dog too gave up then, and lay down, his eyes bloodshot, his head flat along her knees.
— from *Nightwood* by Djuna Barnes

      *   *   *

We in the West have for too long been without passion. Modern man has dedicated himself to the furtherance of civilization — the construction of functional but fragile forms of reality. This impulse has been a significant factor in the extension of consciousness. It has aided us in the difficult task of establishing the perimeter of the rational and scientifically determinable portion of the phenomenal world. It has allowed us to escape from the collective night fears of history's childhood. But all of this and more has been accomplished at an enormous expense by virtue of the fact that it demanded the masculine and "rational" portion of our humanity come to the fore for the task. That is, the immediate and so-called "irrational" response to Being, that which the ancients identified as the Feminine, had to be put aside for us to accomplish what we have. But it is for this very reason that what has been accomplished is sometimes put to ends which lack the wisdom only emotion and passion can give us. In putting aside all that is not "rational," all that does not coincide with the light streaming from the sun of our egos, and in identifying the feminine with the term "irrational," we have buried a portion of ourselves in the gross earth of *avidya*, ignorance. And to make matters worse we have then taken this rash new formulation of the Feminine and identified it with women in general.

The alchemist understood not only the importance of the Feminine within, but also the necessity of attaining a viable relationship with the feminine without, a *soror mystica*, a wife as companion and worker. It was a very simple and unconscious premise, as most truths are: there are two sexes with two fundamentally unique functions. If the world is truly descended from and modelled after a trans-personal sphere, an archetypal dimension devoid of form as we know it, there we may expect to find two pulses of *equal* value — a plus and a minus, a yin and a yang, a systole and a diastole, a contraction and expansion which on this plane has been transcribed into a male and a female.

And here it is important to take note of these differences between the terms masculine/feminine and male/female. The former refer to psychic and spiritual modalities that should never have been *identified* with the latter biological terms.

It is only at this date, in the twentieth century, that the discoveries of the alchemists might be taken and applied. My point is that it is now possible, for the first time, to construct an alchemical yoga of sorts. But the initial risk in outlining such a discipline is in confining its creative and on-going process to fixed rules — and, even more dangerously, to socially determined images of Being. The very nature of alchemy demands that its expression be allowed to modify or amplify different aspects of the work in accordance with the needs or potentials of the worker. This cannot be done if the worker perceives himself or herself as a one-sided figure, fearful of accepting innate qualities because they have been deemed oppositional in nature to the socially prescribed role of the individual.

Ultimately, the alchemical process is Soul work and its aim is the opening of communications between solar and lunar consciousness.

> Know that our work requires a true change of natures, which cannot be unless the union of both these natures becomes absolute. Yet no such union may be, except after the manner of waters . . . this union is not of bodies . . . these do but grind together. . . . Yet of spirits between themselves such union well

may be; but to this end the homogeneous metallic water is required.
—from the *Hermetic Museum*

NOTES

[1]Kerenyi, Karl, *The Religion of the Greeks and Romans*, Greenwood Press Publishers, Westport, Connecticut, 1977, p. 115.

[2]Hillman, James, *Re-Visioning Psychology*, Harper & Row, New York, 1975, p. 140.

ON THE ANDROGYNE

I

Working with symbols is a dangerous business. More often than not our enthusiasm tends to conceal more than it reveals. The imagination that gripped us becomes gripped and slips out of our sight as quicksilver from a clenched fist. The greater the symbol, the greater the danger that this might happen with every interpretive thrust of our inquiry. The pages I am about to create are thick with such dangers, for in the figure of the androgyne we have a symbol almost too large for the meager art of interpretation. I must at the outset admit that what follows is the product of a thing imagined.

The focus of my imagination is the idea that there might be a formula for psychological or spiritual transformation. Its lineaments appear to be given us in religion, myths, spiritual traditions, our dream-life and history as process. The formula is a simple one: at the beginning of every psychological or spiritual process we are presented with a figure composed of the opposites in a state of union; at the middle of the process the opposites exist in a state of division, and at the end of the process the opposites are again united. In religion, mythology, and spiritual disciplines the beginning and end of this process are symbolized by a bi-sexual being.[1] However, because the figure appearing at the beginning is markedly different from that appearing at the end it is imperative that they be labeled and defined. The terms I will employ are familiar: hermaphrodite and androgyne.

There are a number of creation myths in which the establishment and demarcation of the world as we know it comes about through the forceful separation of two World Parents joined in what appears to be an endless state of sexual union. Invariably, we find their offspring angrily suffering the darkness and stasis of their newborn condition. In time, one of the children revolts and gets about the business of separating the pair forever, thereby bringing about all of those circumstances we tend to interpret as symbolic of consciousness: the sun appears, geographic points are established, heaven and earth become fixed locales, speech is invented, and human beings roam the earth. The emphasis these myths place on the tenacity of this couple's embrace and the effort needed finally to separate them, brings to my mind the image of a single bisexual figure, the hermaphrodite.

The special feature of this hermaphroditic creature is the fact that as long as it existed in an undivided state, the world and consciousness could not come into existence. It therefore represents a time that exists prior to the differentiation of psyche and soma. In short, such creation myths may be thought of as illustrating the psychological and biologic nature of the new-born infant. On the one hand, consciousness and the unconscious have not yet been established as two distinct fields, and on the other the recessive qualities of the organism have not yet been separated from the distinguishing biological characteristics of the human body. It was upon this latter reality that Jung based his theory of the anima and the animus:

> It is a well-known fact that sex is determined by a majority of male or female genes, as the case may be. But the minority of genes does not simply disappear. A man therefore has in him a

feminine side, an unconscious feminine figure. . . I have called
this figure the "anima," and its counterpart in a woman the "animus."[2]

We may assume from this that the symbolism of the hermaphrodite in world literature not only refers us to the original
unity of the anima/animus archetypes, but of the masculine and
feminine in ourselves prior to their differentiation. Emphasis is
placed on the genitals in both the archetypal instance, when we
read of the creation myths dealing with the sexual union of the
primal parents, and the biological instance, in which sexual differentiation is established.

The second stage is one in which the original double-sexed
figure is divided. The splitting of the original unity, the T'ai Chi in
Chinese philosophy, also gives birth to the opposites which in turn
make manifest the universe. The sixth day of Genesis brings about
the division of the hermaphroditic Adam into the opposites that
will parent humankind. In every instance the splitting of the hermaphrodite leads to the birth of consciousness and of the world as
we know it.[3] Thus, the price of consciousness is the original unity
of the anima and the animus. The tension that we as humans experience between ourselves and between each other in regard to
the idea of the masculine and the feminine is the wound that we
would heal by realizing their unity.

The third stage in the pattern is symbolized by the opposites re-
united, the major difference being that their union is depicted as
asexual. In religious traditions this figure is always thought of as
an intensification and broadening of our humanity, a time of un-
equivocal freedom symbolized as the result of a marriage sharply
contrasting the sexual union of the hermaphrodite. This is the
androgyne, in Western culture symbolized by the Christ.

We may therefore say that the hermaphroditic state is a given
whereas the androgynous state is a realization. The hermaphrodite
symbolizes the realm of the physical body, the somatic realm that
borders the psyche, whereas the androgyne refers us to the subtle
body and the archetypal realm. The term "hermaphrodite" describes an undesirable state of union, in that it is unconscious and
static, in need of differentiation; while the term "androgyne" corresponds to our myth of a differentiated consciousness comprised
of a union of opposites. And yet Jung warns us that the re-union of
the masculine with the feminine may lead to an extinction of con-

sciousness.[4] Here we reach a difficult juncture for it is often assumed that what is called for is the marriage of our manifest biological nature, with our recessive and psychological nature, which is to say the marriage of the male ego with the anima or the female ego with the animus. Obviously something different must occur. The myth that all we need do is marry ourselves to what is recessive in us falls apart when we read Jung's comment that the sacred marriage, and therefore the androgynous process,[5] does not take place "within the sphere of discriminating consciousness."[6]

> The anima and animus live in a world quite different from the world outside — in a world where the pulse of time beats infinitely slowly, where the birth and death of individuals count for little.[7]

The desire in anima and animus to take part in the world of consciousness that has been created through their separation, places upon us the responsibility of providing a proper stage for their manifestation. We might imagine that the interplay of these two archetypal figures gives shape to the soul in much the same manner that the interplay of the male and female in the world gives shape to our existence in the body. The more attention that we give to the construction of a proper stage setting, the greater the effect that the archetypes have on us, for ultimately it is their interaction that creates the drama and the comedy of our lives. Jung's statement that the union of these divine opposites occurs outside of consciousness implies that it is not my 'I-ness' as a male that must marry the archetype, but rather the conjunction of the animus with the anima. But if men have access only to the anima, and women only to the animus, how then are we to effect such a union — wherever such a union may occur? James Hillman noted this discrepancy in two papers on the anima which I feel clear up some major difficulties.

Simply put, Hillman states that the restricting of the anima to men and the animus to women is not tenable in the light of pure observation. The characteristics of the anima thought to be available only to men appear in women as well.[8] In addition, he points out that by restricting the concept of anima or of soul to men alone is to do nothing more than to maintain the traditional view that women are without soul, every image that would be defined as anima in a man's experience ending up as shadow in a woman's.[9]

The upshot of his observation is that the animus and the anima, or at least their effects, are equally available to both men and women. This somewhat helps us out of our difficulty—a conjunction of the anima/animus now theoretically possible within the area of one soul. It is no longer just a matter of the man's anima hooking up with a woman's animus. It can be that too, but it is clearly not *just* that.

It also helps to clear up another difficulty I believe must have plagued any number of people involved with Jungian ideas. Here I refer to the fact that while Jung often employed the symbolism of Chinese philosophy and Kundalini yoga to transpose his observations into psychological theory, the fact that these systems speak of the masculine (yang/Shiva) and feminine (yin/Shakti) as contained in both sexes did nothing to alter profoundly the one-archetype-to-one-sex theory. Hillman's reading of Jung and his redefining of the anima/animus theory finds support in the texts of ancien: philosophy. The stumbling block to our perception of the sacred marriage and the androgyne comes simply from the problem of our transposing it into terms of ego and archetype, physical and transpersonal, I and that which is without 'I-ness.' All of which leads us to the next question: If the androgyne is not a happening in the field of ego-consciousness, where is it happening?

Jung tells us that the sacred marriage takes place in the alchemical substance Mercurius[10] and he adds that Mercurius is the hermaphroditic or bisexual figure that stands at both the beginning and the end of the alchemical process, that it is at once the prima materia and the philosopher's stone.[11] In other words, according to our definition, Mercurius is the hermaphrodite *and* the androgyne. In addition, he identifies Mercurius as the collective unconscious, the place of archetypal reality that at every moment impinges upon our world as we live it. Thus, the transformation of our hermaphroditic natures, as well as the healing of the split caused by the advent of consciousness, takes place *in* the androgyne. The androgyne is pre-existent. It is not something we create any more than we create the Mother or the Hero archetype. It is. If anything it creates us and we in our divided state can only hope to enter into participation with it through some type of method as yet not collectively perceived. The androgyne is a truly transpersonal reality, a subtle body whose existence must be awakened to.

To discover the geography of the androgyne we must first consider that Jung came to doubt the "exclusively psychic nature of the archetypes," finding them to have a nature that "cannot with certainty be designated as psychic."[12]

> . . . the archetypes are not found exclusively in the psychic sphere, but can occur just as much in circumstances that are not psychic (equivalence of an outward physical process with a psychic one).[13]

If the archetypal world is not confined to the human soul but extends throughout the continuum of being and non-being, then we are faced with the fact that the experience of the androgyne as a subjective happening — the identification of myself as a happy union of masculine and feminine qualities — is illusory if it is not accompanied by a simultaneous occurrence of archetypally-toned phenomena in the world about me. That the similarity of such phenomena is a necessary adjunct to the activation of an archetype is the basis of Jung's definition of synchronicity.[14] The uniqueness of Jung's perception concerning the nature of synchronicity has in a way served to blind us to the simple reality of his theory. If I am present to a moment of synchronicity, a meaningful coincidence in which inner and outer worlds correspond, I am then contained in something different from the everyday world of consciousness. Henry Corbin puts us on to the situation in greater detail:

> Spiritual [i.e. archetypal or imaginal] bodies or entities are not *in* any world, nor *in* their world, in the same manner as a material body is in its place or may be contained in another body. On the contrary, their world is *in* them. . . Of course, all these entities subsist independently of each other. Nonetheless, all exist simultaneously and each is contained in the other.[15]

In other words, the activation of the androgyne is a moment in which we become contained in an androgynous world. What happens is that we then become capable of perceiving the androgyne, and it is the perception of this world that allows us the effect of the androgyne which in turns opens us to the possibility of such a consciousness.[16] I emphasize that it is solely a possibility, for the entry into the mercurial waters of the archetype becomes a revelatory happening in consciousness only if one can allow that everyday realities are penetrated through and through by archetypes — that, in the words of Evangelos Christou, "The psyche is not inside man, it is we who are inside the psyche."[17] James Joyce attempted to alert us to this reality by having his hero, Leopold Bloom, live out the entire cycle of Ulysses' travels during the passage of one day. The comedy and tragedy of Bloom is that he never fully realizes that he moves in the midst of an archetypal world, that he himself has become the myth. So too do many of us float in our myths, the symbol of the androgyne being but one of many archetypes in a series of archetypal awakenings. William James suggested that human consciousness is one of many worlds.[18] These other worlds of consciousness are the archetypes.

> . . . the unseen region in question is not merely ideal, for it produces effects in this world. When we commune with it, work is actually done upon our finite personality, for we are turned into new men. . . But that which produces effects within another reality must be termed a reality itself . . .[19]

So what we are discussing is the problem of perceiving ourselves *in* the androgyne. We must somehow become capable of seeing through the opaqueness of ego-consciousness and into the realm of archetypal happenings, or perceiving that the symbol, the image, is a world of consciousness in its own right and not something that we create out of hand. I do not mean to imply by the foregoing, however, that this suggested imaginal three-fold processes of transformation solely occurs in the archetypal realm. I am on the side of the Chinese who say that the process of becoming manifests itself through the world of humanity (inter-personal relationships), earth (the demands of being-in-the-world), and heaven (the archetypal or imaginal realm).[20]

At the interpersonal level, for example, when two people come together in love in a way that causes an inexpressible feeling of romantic oneness to encompass and contain them both, we can assume that they have entered the hermaphroditic world. Their immersion in each other to the exclusion of their individual differences (which as we all know are put aside at such moments), blurs the person. The urge of the anima and animus to unite in one body draws us out of ourselves and into a conjunction through which our souls attempt to find their other halves outside of us in projected form. In time the projection begins to fade and we slowly and painfully notice the all too human differences that exist between ourselves and those who have received our projection. Such projections, in turn, tend to become prisons for the recipient. Suddenly demands are made to fulfill the soul-image projected upon us and we rebel, separate; we suddenly find ourselves in the midst of divisive issues where once there had been total agreement and unity. The second phase of the process has begun and its successful completion is dependent upon the integrity, consciousness, and emotional capacity of each party finally to perceive one another outside of the hermaphroditic world. That such separations inevitably occur suggests that the androgyne cannot be realized until the withdrawal of our soul-projections are realized. When I know where I begin and end and where the other person begins and ends, then I and the other are on the way to the world of the androgyne.

In the meantime the withdrawal of my projection leads me towards conflicting doubts about the nature and reality of my soul in general — "How could I have fallen in love with such a person?" we ask. This expulsion from the Paradise of the hermaphrodite signals the first step towards a consciousness of our situation. If one can sustain the tension of growing out of this separation the inward pull of the withdrawn projection eventually leads us towards the other half of the soul within us for entry into the androgynous world. What this means in the area of relationships is that whereas in the hermaphroditic phase of our coming together there was one, in the androgynous phase there are three — two individuals and the third thing that unites them in consciousness.[21]

By the same token, at the level of our relationships with the business of being-in-the-world, I can become hermaphroditic, individual, and androgynous in regard to my job, my ideas, even my pastimes. We are all familiar with the businessman or the housewife who become identified with their jobs to the exclusion of themselves as individuals.

It goes without saying that political, sociological, and psychological approaches to the world of the androgyne will effect change in our social philosophies. In the long run such platforms will have little effect on our souls if the archetype itself is not dealt with in what Corbin has defined as the realm of the imaginal, where the image resides. For this, he adds, one must call upon the aid of an "organ of trans-sensory imagination."[22] In that Jung said that the basis of all consciousness is the image,[23] entry into the world of the androgyne demands that each of us perform an active imagination over the nature of our interiority as well as the archetypal ground that everywhere surrounds us. It is there, in the imaginal, where the androgyne resides, and it is there where we must journey if we are to bring ourselves to a consciousness that may truly be called androgynous.

But we have several problems to overcome, for ever since the close of the seventeenth century, and certainly ever since the advent of modern psychology, we have had a deep-seated fear of confusing the imaginal with the ego-world—and not without good reason I must add. What has happened, however, is that we presently have psychologies that seek to cut us off from the imaginal, to make us wholly conscious, invulnerable to imagination and the archetypes.

But invulnerability means that one cannot be touched, and if one cannot be touched one cannot be psychologically moved. The fear of the imaginal becomes a pathology in itself, a withdrawal of the ego from all that is dark, unknown, and sensual in favor of that which is light, distant and above-it-all, in control. Ego-consciousness is won at the price of depth of soul. What is peculiar to humanity—its awareness of suffering, its pathos and its comedy, its ability to endure the sometimes painful reality of Being—becomes coated over by a myth of happiness-is-healthiness. The intrusion of images and phantasies onto the screen of consciousness becomes something we should rid ourselves of, in true yogic fashion. Consciousness becomes equated with not only happiness but psychic blankness. My nightmares should be ignored and my anxieties tranquilized. The mental clinic becomes a place where people are corrected rather than connected or understood. I am told that if I want to get in touch with my anger (and therefore with something that is primal and connects me with the base of psyche) I should use a punching bag, or become verbally abusive to my wife, my employer, my children. Action replaces perception.

But none of the prescriptions given us today by either psychology, religion, philosophy or even a good friend puts us in contact with the androgyne. The only thing that puts us in contact with that archetype is the very thing everyone tries to cure us of—the conflict of the opposites in their divisive state. What we have not yet fully developed is a method by which we may finally marry the opposites again, safely.

I have reached the end of my first imagining, the major attempt of which was to suggest a definition of the terms hermaphrodite and androgyne, propose that there exists a threefold process of psychological transformation, repeat the oft-stated policy that there are indeed other worlds of consciousness, and imply that where there is another world of consciousness, there must also be another method for the attainment of that consciousness.

II

Tantric tradition tells us that prior to the creation of all things the Great Lord Shiva existed in his unmanifest form of Parashiva, void of all distinctions. Contained within this sexless first principle were an inactive principle that would in time come to be regarded as the father of the universe, and an active principle that would become known as the mother.[24] But this ever-changeless Being had a *Kama* (desire) to be an ever-changing seeming and thereby took on the role of relative becoming. As one text tells us, this *Kama* gave rise to the active feminine principle, the Primordial Shakti, who in adoration of Her Lord turned herself into a "Pure mirror in which Shiva experiences Himself."[25] Upon this mirror fell the rays of Parashiva as the sun. The substance of these rays, inactive in itself, was then carried by the energic-reflection of the Shakti, each reflection causing a diminution of the Divine feminine, to create a series of worlds, or tattvas of which there are thirty-six. This series of manifestations are understood as the *"stages of evolution of the One into the Many as Mind and matter"*.[26] With the manifestation of the 36th tattva, the earth, Shakti's creativity came to a close as she, in the form of a serpent, entered the grossness of matter to sleep. In this form the feminine is known as Kundalini-Sakti, and the Earth that she slumbers in is the human body.[27] In such a manner does the microcosm come into being. The macrocosm (*Mahabramanda*), composed of the sacred mountain Meru and fourteen worlds — of which seven are imagined as upper, and seven as nether or lower — is the model for the human body. Mt. Meru is the spinal column and the seven upper worlds become seven centers or chakras located along its length. The seven nether worlds are imagined as existing below the first chakra (the *muladhara*) "and in the joints, sides, anus, and organs of generation".[28] The personal soul (*purusha*) we are told corresponds with the cosmic soul (*Hiranyagarbha*).

It is believed the life force of the individual is dispersed through

the two channels of *Ida* and *Pingala*, the moon and the sun channels respectively.[29] We may think of these channels as symbolic of
Eros and Logos. The sun channel may be imagined as symbolizing
either an extraverted and dispassionate manner of dealing with the
world or as the source of volatile impulses. By the same token, the
moon channel may be imagined as symbolizing either an introverted and impassioned manner of dealing with the world or as the
source of corrosive compulsions. The object of Kundalini yoga is
to liberate oneself from the unconscious activities of the sun and
the moon channels by withdrawing the energy contained within
them. The retrieved energies are then shuttled up the central channel with the aid of Kundalini.[30] The withdrawal of these energies
activates the sleeping serpent causing it to rise up through the central channel, activating and purifying the chakras until it enters
into a sacred union with the masculine principle.[31]

Anyone who has ever entered into a yogic regimen will readily
admit that what has been described above is no mere illusion. The
psychological effects of this discipline are pronounced as are the
many psychic disturbances that sometimes arise. But the most
curious thing about this yoga is not that there are effects, but that
the entire process begins *through an assiduous application of imagination*. Practically the whole of the Yoga Upanishads[32] concerns itself with the description of what is to be internally *seen* by
the yogin in his practice. It is not without interest to note that the
creation of the world in Tantricism is spoken of as a product of
creative imagination. We are told that Shiva and Shakti represent
the static and kinetic aspects of consciousness and that the power
that brings the dualistic world into being, Maya-Sakti, is actually a
veiling and projecting principle.[33] It is for this reason that the
world is called an imagination (*Kalpana*) and Shakti is imagined as
a consciousness that imagines (*Srsti-kalpana*) the world into being.
The dualistic world comes into being through a process of Creative
Imagination. Thus entry into the world of the subtle body and the
Androgyne is accomplished through the feminine, the Shakti/
Anima. It is important to remember that Tantric myth tells us the
world came into existence through the agency of the anima as mirror, as reflector. We must also call to mind Jung's statement that
the instincts fall into five major groups: hunger, sexuality, activity, creativity, and reflection.[34] About this latter instinct he
wrote, "Reflection is the cultural instinct *par excellence*, and its

strength is shown in the power of culture to maintain itself in the
face of untamed nature."[35] Jung's reasons for identifying reflection
as an instinct are as follows: the instinct of activity, or rather its
drive, is in humans transfered by a moment of deliberation or reflection before its carry-over into action. At least, this is the idealized state of humanity. We train our dogs into mimicking something like a state of reflection that cause them to go against their
instinctual impulse to attack with commands such as "sit" or "halt."
But true reflection is a specifically human instinct and one that the
Tantric texts inform us is an innate activity of the anima. Jung said
much the same:[36]

> Where judgements and flashes of insight are transmitted by un-
> conscious activity, they are often attributed to an archetypal
> feminine figure, the anima or mother-beloved.[37]

Also: "The richness of the human psyche and its essential character are probably determined by this reflective instinct."[38] To
which Hillman adds, "This psyche is mainly a result of the instinct
of reflection, which in turn is intimately tied with the anima archetype," and quoting from Jung again:

> . . . reflection is a spiritual act that runs counter to the natural
> process; an act whereby we stop, call something to mind, form a
> picture, and take up a relation to and come to terms with what
> we have seen. It should, therefore, be understood as an act of be-
> coming conscious.[39]

Wrapping it up for our purposes here, one final quote from
Hillman:

> If 'becoming conscious' has its roots in reflection and if this in-
> stinct refers to the anima archetype, then consciousness itself
> may more appropriately be conceived as based upon anima than
> upon ego.[40]

What is truly curious is that all of these very learned psychological statements and observations are contained in our Tantric
myth. The human world, and thus human consciousness, comes
into being through a reflective act on the part of the Shakti/
Anima. In addition, each chakra is thought of as governing one of
the senses[41] and therefore symbolic of *a* consciousness, so the call
for the repeated passage of the Kundalini/anima through these
centers suggests that the anima is behind our sensory appreciation

of the world — behind our very "earthiness." But the implications
do not end here if we recall that the Tantric text calls for an image
of the Parasiva figure to become located in the head of humans, its
model being the Macrocosmic Parasiva. This microcosmic
Parasiva becomes the ego of Western psychology which Jung tells
us is but a small model of the Self.[42]

The Shiva/ego is therefore an unreflective aspect of consciousness that is incapable of perceiving itself without the intervention
of the Shakti/anima's appearance as reflector. Without reflection
and imagination the ego's perception of the world is without substance, airy. Jung put it nicely when he wrote that "Matter represents the concreteness of God's thoughts,"[43] for religious
tradition tells us that the feminine *is* matter. Without reflection
there is no substance, without anima there is only a blank seeing.
Therefore ego-consciousness alone cannot lead us to the realization of the androgyne. Because the androgyne is composed of
both the masculine and feminine, it demands a masculine and a
feminine consciousness to perceive it. Reflection and imagination
are the trans-sensory organs of the perception that Corbin observed is needed for a greater consciousness.

We must now consider the statements given us concerning the
manifestation of the Shakti through the worlds. Hindu commen-
tators call this activity of the Shakti/anima a dimming of Shiva
consciousness in that the rays of Shiva's body become clothed with
the Mayanic energy of the feminine. Consciousness is equated
with the masculine and unconsciousness with the feminine — a
thesis in no way peculiar to modern Western psychology also, as
unsettling as it must be to women. The final act in the creation
myth leaves us with the image of the depleted feminine tucked
away at the base of the human body. I suggest that the glorious descriptions of Kundalini's beauty given us by the Hindu not detract
us from the fact that the feminine has essentially become at this
point a sleeping beauty of the alimentary zones. A number of religious traditions in the West also tell us of a spiritual masculine
principle residing on high, in a fixed position of centrality, from
which the feminine has become separated. The Gnosticism of
Justin informs us that the creator of the universe, Elohim, deserted
his wife Eden so that he could ascend towards a light brighter than
the sun. The desertion brings about a desire for revenge on his
wife's part that leads to the human ills of adultery, general sin, and

evil to flourish on the earth with which she is (as the Kundalini) identified.[44]

Yet another doctrine, that of Simon, has it that the First Thought, that which leaped towards the nether regions to create the world after the plan of her Father's will, was held captive on ea⁻·h by the angels and powers she created. She in time suffers the fi⸱al humiliation by becoming trapped in a human body to undergo numerous incarnations, "Always suffering disgrace from it . . . until she was manifest in a prostitute."[45] The myth of Jewish mysticism, Kabbalism, has it that the feminine portion of God, the Shekhinah, is trapped in the lower of four worlds (*asiyah*) where only evil spirits and mankind dwell. As in the Gnostic and Tantric myth, she too is symbolized by and identified with the earth.

The major feature of all these myths (and others too numerous to recount here) is that the dimming of the bright light of consciousness (as in the Tantric myth) is brought about by the creation of the human world, and is in one way or another the cause of the feminine. The suggestion in all of these myths is that the Divine business cannot be completed until the feminine returns to the sphere of the masculine, and return under her own power, no less. If we consider these myths in our imaginal formula for transformation, the separation out of the hermaphroditic state that brings about consciousness, the opposites, and individuality occurs because of the feminine. *But this occurrence is seen as a fault.* The masculine rejects the whole affair out of hand and goes about its immovable centeredness. It is as if every gain in ego-consciousness must be countered by a pulling away from and rejection of the imaginative and reflective qualities of the anima. The masculine is content merely to perceive the suffering that these many myths inform us the anima undergoes in her exile. Jung, commenting upon a similar depiction of the Sophia in yet another Gnostic tale, notes that such a condition clearly characterizes "the anima of a man who identifies himself absolutely with his reason and his spirituality."[46] The inevitable result of this is a dissociation from the anima and the compensatory healing powers of the unconscious in general, thereby cutting himself off from, "on the one hand the anima as the connecting link with the world beyond and the eternal images, while on the other hand her emotionality which involves man in the chthonic world and its transitoriness."[47]

The fixity of the masculine in all of these myths, the demand that the feminine get herself out of her predicament, means that the masculine "is content to merely perceive psychic suffering, but does not make itself conscious of the reasons behind it."[48]

What we are faced with is a predicament in which the birth of consciousness also causes a displacement and depreciation of the very thing that gave rise to it. These ancient myths reveal the attitude towards the unconscious that consciousness would eventually take. In turn, the rejection of the anima in our psyches becomes the rejection of the female in the world. We should also consider that these myths anticipated if not predicted the predicament of twentieth-century consciousness. If this is indeed the case, then we must be able to discover somewhere in these imaginal systems the next development in consciousness, or at the very least the nature of our present condition at the collective level.

The estrangement of the anima from the animus is depicted in the Kundalini system by the figure of the slumbering Kundalini in the *muladhara* chakra. In the Kabbalistic system of the Sefiroth, we also discover that the Shekhinah is essentially unconscious in that she lives in a world of evil darkness. In both instances the home of the feminine is the element earth. The upward movement these feminine principles must undertake represents the third phase in our imaginal process of transformation only in that it is a step towards union. Archetypally speaking, this is a movement towards the world of the androgyne. But before we can begin an attempt to see if we may indeed discover where we are in terms of these two imaginal systems it would do us well to consider some observations that Jung made concerning the Chakra system.[49]

Jung first turns our attention to the second chakra to suggest that its symbolism of ocean and sea-monster answers our twentieth-century Western description of the unconscious. He goes on to say that this second chakra might therefore be called "the chakra or mandala of baptism, or of rebirth, or of destruction, whatever the consequence of baptism might be."[50] In other words, it symbolizes everything that happens to us when we meet the unconscious. Then he turns his attention to the first chakra, (*muladhara*), and asks us to reconsider its symbolism.

Identifying the second chakra as the unconscious is a fairly simple matter, for it contains all of the elements symbolic of the night-sea journey, but the first chakra presents some problems in that a Westerner would immediately assume it too symbolizes the unconscious. Its element is earth, its name is the "root support," it contains a phallus and slumbering serpent, and it is a symbol of what *is* unconscious. But what *is* unconscious isn't necessarily *the* unconscious. The symbolism tells us that with this chakra "we are in the region of the roots of our existence on this earth."[51] In other words, muladhara is the earth mandala and represents "where mankind is a victim of impulses, instincts, unconsciousness . . . *participation mystique*."[52] What is unconscious in this mandala is not *the* unconscious but the Self.

This leads to the possibility that muladhara is located in our heads and not in the perianal region: that the entire chakra system becomes inverted in the West.[53] Thus the idea that the second chakra is below us rather than above us (as in the Eastern system) corresponds with the psychological facts of the Western world: the way to the unconscious is down not up, in not out.[54] Jung's re-alignment of the Chakra system fits in with everything that we have said about the condition of the feminine at the apogee of her separation from the masculine. The world she slumbers in is indeed the unconscious of the Gods and it is not until the feminine is awakened that the possibility of their recognition as vital factors in humanity might again come to pass. It is through the faculty of a re-awakened active and creative imagination that we might again come into contact with the imaginal.

In the light of Jung's statement identifying the first chakra — and therefore the first sefirah of the Kabbalistic system as well — with the unconscious, let us now consider the next point of reference. That the first chakra and the first sefirah coincide is an interesting coincidence at first sight. A close look at the coincidence of the Svadhisthana chakra and the Yesod sefirah leads us into deeper waters. Both are symbolized by the genitals and both represent the first attempt at a reconciliation of the opposites. If the muladhara chakra is indeed located in the head, in the field of our everyday Western consciousness, and if the myth of estrangement from the anima is aptly depicted in our masculine attitude towards the unconscious and the anima, then what does it mean that the unconscious in both of these systems is identified by the genitals? What is there about the twentieth-century psyche that in any way corresponds with this symbolism?

Consider this: if there is any one idea that has changed the whole of twentieth-century thought right down to the awareness of the high school freshman, if there is any one myth that has gripped the imagination of the entire civilized Western world, it is the myth of this ephemeral thing we call the unconscious. The myth of the unconscious represents the first awakening of the Kundalini/anima in that it called forth every ounce of Western imagination to accept it as a philosophical probability. With the advent of this theory the movement towards the androgyne began. It was only fitting that we should move towards the imaginal with an imaginal concept. Consider this further: *the* prominent myth of the unconscious today, that which every housewife and businessman, laborer, scholar, and philosopher could name without fail on any quiz show is the Freudian myth. It would therefore profit us to take a brief look at Freud within the context of everything we have said up to this point.

Freud came to the realization of one of his most important contributions through his dissatisfaction with the technique of hypnotic suggestion.[55] In his attempt to deal with the problem of post-hypnotic amnesia, he persuaded his patients to free-associate by closing their eyes and concentrating on memory recall. Conscious associations were to be put aside in favor of the spontaneous images that came to mind. In other words, he intuited that the way into the unconscious was through imagining — for every memory comes to us via the image. If any of us should attempt to remember what it was that we had for supper two evenings ago we would have to rely on an imagining of the meal — on a "seeing" of the past. The act of free-association thereby came to define the psychiatric process. The time spent with my analyst was a time spent imagining. The creation of the space called a psychoanalytic hour came into existence through the type of reflection we saw Shakti perform in creating the world. The world of my analysis is created through the activity of the anima imagining, through the feminine reflecting what will in time become the substance of not only my analysis but myself as well.

The next important observation that Freud made was that within every neurosis there were to be found delusional phantasies, i.e. imaginings, and that it is these phantasies themselves that give rise to symptoms of both a physiological and physical nature.[56] The source of all such phantasies we are told is the masturbatory phase of childhood.[57] And, finally, all symptoms have their origin in "the expression of both a masculine and a feminine unconscious sexual phantasy," or what he referred to as a bisexual nature.[58] In other words, the proddings of the phantasies behind a neurosis might be likened to the proddings of those children in our creation myths who attempt to bring about the separation of their hermaphroditic parents. The separation of my ego from the compulsive aspect of the unconscious leads to a consciousness of who and what I am. The bi-sexual activity Freud referred to may be likened to the hermaphroditic being composed of the anima and the animus prior to their separation. Every neurosis is a hermaphrodite attempting to become an androgyne.

The framework within which Freud worked appears to be even more archetypal than we tend to recognize when we consider his theory of libido. In *An Outline of Psychoanalysis*, he writes that there are two basic instincts, Eros and the destructive instinct, which he later called Thanatos.[59] He tells us that the aim of Eros — which he quickly renames libido[60] — "is to establish ever greater unities and to preserve them thus — in short, to bind together."[61]

The expression of this libido, furthermore, streams into the ego "from the various organs and parts of the body,"[62] the most prominent portions called the erotogenic zones. Strictly speaking, he adds, the entire body is an erotogenic zone.[63] The technique of psychoanalysis is one of freeing up libido which has flowed back to an early stage of human development. The regression of this "life force" was thought of by him as the cause of psychic illness.

Eros, or what Freud came to call libido, was according to two Greek accounts the first God to appear after the creation of the primal parents. He was to the Greek mind what he was in part to Freud, the cement of the world. In the same manner that he appears at the beginning of the world in Greek mythology, so too may he be thought of as being actively present in muladhara. He is both the blinding and binding force that keeps us rooted in the world. *Participation mystique* is a phenomenon of Eros. To fall in step with a collective mood is to fall in Love with that mood. Falling *in* love means just that — becoming encompassed by the archetype. This great, powerful, and all encompassing God of the Greeks in time became the infantile Cupid of Roman and modern times. The power of loving and its full expression became reduced to the capricious past-time, the masturbatory myth personified, of the infant. It is this end of the myth that Freud emphasized in his theory of the libido. In that theory, Eros is no longer a divine archetypal power that grips us, he is a compulsive seeking of pleasure that must undergo a process of maturation.

Here we have the myth complete. The maturation process is one in which libido becomes centered in and passes through three erotogenic zones: the mouth, the anus, and the penis, in that order. All three zones are described as "sexual" in that pleasure in one form or another is obtained from them during the development of the child.[64] The oral, anal, and phallic phases of maturation come to a close during early childhood to later give place to the genital phase of puberty. A further point of interest is that in the phallic phase "what comes in question . . . is not the genitals of both sexes but only those of the male. . . The female genitals long remain unknown."[65] This is a remarkable statement—the implication that the female child is more aware of the phallus than the reality of her own body. The fact that Freud who had much to say about our infantile origins never analyzed a child[66] can suggest only that such a treatment arose out of an imagining about the mythical or archetypal nature of things that he then literally applied to psychology in general.[67]

I strongly feel that the theory of libido and its development through the oral, anal, and phallic phases all have their origin in the archetypal configuration given us in the first chakra of Kundalini yoga. It is in that chakra where the totally unconscious nature of the Kundalini is symbolized by the image of her mouth encircling the susumna channel while her body itself lies entwined around a phallus. The location of this chakra—between the anus and the genitals—completes our Freudian picture. The final phase of maturation that Freud spoke of, the genital phase in which the sexual organs of both male and female are realized rather than the phallic alone, corresponds with the localization of the second chakra in the genital area. It is here too that the free-association method, the activation of unconscious contents, finds correspondence.

If nothing else Freud was called to the archetype to begin the modern myth-making process of transformation. His psychology of the genitals was a fulfillment of a development in the stages of consciousness intimated in the anthropomorphic figures of the Sefirothic and Kundalini Yoga systems. The revelation that the psyche gave us in the guise of a threefold system of transformation was as follows: first there will come to pass the myth of a world without archetypes that will then become a reality through the fashioning of a culture and a consciousness that thoroughly entertains this viewpoint, a mulhadharic consciousness. The historian of religions Mircea Eliade has commented upon this event in the following:

> It should be said at once that the completely profane world, the wholly desacralized cosmos, is a recent discovery in the history of the human spirit. . . Desacralization pervades the entire experience of the nonreligious man of modern societies and . . . in consequence, he finds it increasingly difficult to rediscover the existential dimensions of religious man in the archaic societies."[68]

This desacralization of the world, the death of God announced only a few short years ago in our weeklies, appears to be a necessary stage in the evolution of consciousness. Yet, our threefold model of transformation informs us that with the arrival of a consciousness that explains itself in terms of the symbolism of the genitals as well as the idea of the superiority of the masculine and the inferiority of the feminine, there will begin a movement towards the androgynic world.

We earlier discussed the idea that it is more a matter of entering the world of an archetype than it is of constellating an archetype within us. At that time I stressed that everything about oneself takes on the tone of the archetype in question. This is what has happened to us through the vehicle of Freudian theories. Our world is now encompassed by the Freudian myth of Oedipal conflicts, anality, penis envy, and the inferiority of both the feminine and the female. Much of the blame for our condition is heaped on the head of Freud rather than on our own heads for failing to perceive that what now grips us is the very thing that gripped him: an archetypal process of transformation whose value and meaning can be perceived only through a constant awareness of the androgyne as a symbol of a final becoming, as a symbol of a final development of consciousness. That history continually presents us with this androgynic figure as exemplary of a completion (right up to the present religious figure of the androgynous Christ) should have alerted us long ago.

I close my second imagining with the following observations: the mythic systems of the Sefiroth in Kabbalism and Kundalini Yoga in Tantricism display a process of becoming within the framework of an anthropomorphic figure. This figure is at once symbolic of an imaginal transpersonal body and our own bodies. Contained therein are stages that define the development of consciousness not only along subjective lines, but along historical and collective lines as well. In addition, we may assume that the appearance of this anthropomorphic figure in history may have coincided with the establishment of consciousness at the collective and evolutionary level. Thus the figure is a method that the psyche has given us for perceiving the manner by which the opposites that were divided at the birth of consciousness may again be united. Finally, the appearance of psychology as a science of psyche indicates that for the first time since the emergence of the phenomenon of human consciousness a movement towards the union of these opposites has begun. All that is needed is a re-evaluation of the feminine in ourselves and the female in the world. Without this, the experiment of psyche will fail.

III

Kundalini yoga was obviously one attempt on the part of the psyche to present us with an imaginal psychology — a method by which we could enter the world of the archetypes and participate in the spiritual and evolutionary character of the psyche first-hand. In contrast with many of our twentieth-century psychologies that deal with the Shiva aspect of consciousness — the extension of consciousness from a fixed center, the development of ego, the strengthening of personality — Kundalini yoga appears to concern itself with the dynamics of soul: with imagination, with psychic deepening, with unity, the body, and God. Jung was much attracted to this science of the soul and often made reference to it stating that there existed amazing parallels between it and his experience with the Western psyche. Yet, he warned us against actively applying a method with foreign roots on many occasions.[69] The fact that such similarities were found by Jung indicates that the West could easily develop an imaginal psychology similar in construction to Kundalini yoga. Jung wrote:

> In the course of the centuries the West will produce its own yoga, and it will be on the basis laid down by Christianity. It is more than likely that the yoga natural to the European proceeds from historical patterns unknown to the East.[70]

Charles Poncé

I now turn your attention back to Jung's comments concerning the nature of the chakra systems in the West. Muladhara, the chakra of the rejected and slumbering Kundalini/anima, is for us located in the field of our consciousness, in the domain of the ego-world. The suggestion is that our mundane view of psyche traps the anima in the field of ego. Her original reflective power has been diminished and parodied by the ego in the think-tank type of reflection we too often pass off as creative thinking. But true creative thinking the myths tell us cannot come to pass without the operations of the anima as reflector. Yet, the myth of modern consciousness tells us that the feminine is not only abased but without power. We therefore find the Freudian myth informing us that women are incapable of developing a strong superego — a theory created in an attempt to explain the then prevailing view that women naturally have a weak moral nature.[71] The original Jungian view that the anima is available only to men did little to help correct the matter, I must add.[72]

This image of the reflective feminine contained and imprisoned by the masculine, swallowed up and limited by ego, is given us in one of the myths of Zeus. We are told that Zeus was warned that the daughter of Okeanus, Metis, whom he had taken as a mistress, would one day give birth to a child or something stronger than his lightning. In the hope of circumventing his fate, Zeus swallowed Metis, trapping her in his stomach. What he didn't know was that she was pregnant and that the cause of his severe headaches shortly afterwards was the issue of their union seeking to be born. Aid was brought with the plunging of a double-ax into his head to release — armour shining like a thousand suns — the goddess Athena.

If one recalls Jung's statement to the effect that the ego is but a small model of the Self, also keeping in mind the Tantric belief that the Parasiva has its duplicate in the world, in our heads, then Zeus might be seen as a perfect model for the Western Ego. Argumentative, ready to strike down all who go against his wishes, seducer, and supreme judge, Zeus in these aspects fits in many ways the description of what goes on in the Western offices of power. It is here that we find the daughter of Metis ("wise counsel"), of insight and reflection, banging at the door of ego-consciousness to get out.

Athena was known as the goddess who gave courage to the warrior, who replaced passion with reason and reflection thereby causing many a hero to put up his sword rather than impulsively strike. Whereas her mother symbolized practical understanding, she represents illuminating clarity. She therefore brings another dimension of perception to the masculine through reflection. Myth tells us that it was only his gazing at the reflection of the Medusa in his shield that saved Perseus from becoming petrified. The shield is a symbol of Athena and the myth suggests that the petrifying quality that the unconscious sometimes holds for consciousness can be overcome only through the anima's gift of reflection. As Walter Otto has described Athena, she is "the heavenly presence and direction as illumination and inspiration to victorious comprehension and consummation."[73]

In Kundalini yoga the arrival of the Kundalini in the sixth chakra and her union with Shiva, the sacred marriage, releases a flood of ambrosia that anoints and illuminates the interior of the body, or psyche. I would like to suggest that the splitting open of the head of Zeus and the brilliance accompanying the emergence of Athena symbolize the same moment — the release of this feminine principle of reflection, and therefore the completion of an androgynic consciousness. But if in the Tantric system of Kundalini yoga it is the feminine that travels upward to meet the masculine, what then is it that travels upwards in our system to liberate the feminine?

We have already indicated that the ajna chakra, because of the inversion of the chakra system in our psyches, ends up where muladhara should be, in the genital zone. It was also implied that the Shiva principle who resides in that chakra becomes localized in that zone. If indeed our Kundalini/anima may be identified as Athena, who then might be identified with the Shiva? I return to the East for one final myth.

Vishnu, "the anthropomorphic embodiment of this fluid of life,"[74] is found floating in his own essence when he sees another luminous apparition approaching him at a great speed. There suddenly stands before him the "fashioner of the universe," Brahma, who immediately asks the reclining God who he is. Vishnu explains that he is the creator and destroyer of the universe. Brahma retorts that he is, and not Vishnu. As the two argue there suddenly appears out of the ocean an enormous lingam crowned with flame. It grows into infinity. Neither Brahma nor Vishnu can see the beginning or end of this phallus. They decide to investigate.

Vishnu plunges downward in the form of a boar and Brahma flies
upward in the shape of a gander. They can find no end to the lingam. Suddenly it bursts open to reveal the great Lord Shiva who
proclaims that he is the origin of them both, Super-shiva "the triad
of Brahma, Vishnu, and Shiva."[75] Thus the phallus and Shiva symbolize the creative masculine principle of the universe — which
"procreates and sustains the universe."[76] He is therefore not only
the creator, but the active spiritual principle in nature. In Greek
mythology three Gods are represented by the phallus, one of them
symbolizing the active and dynamic principle in nature — the great
god Pan who is in several ways connected with the other two
phallic Gods Dionysus and Hermes.

The phallic nature of the god Hermes appears to have arisen
from his depiction as god of the stone-heap, *herma*. Herms, later
replaced with ithyphallic busts of the God, were employed as
markers along paths and crossroads. Hermes himself was regarded
as "the friendliest of gods to men,"[77] bestower of fruitfulness,
shepherd of the flocks, and the guide to the underworld. Today he
might be thought of as a guide to the unconscious. Myth tells us
that he fell in love with a nymph who in time gave birth to their
son Pan. Pan means "All," a name given him by the gods because
the goat-footed and horned child pleased them all. He pleased the
God Dionysus so much that the latter took the young Goat-god
into his service. Pan we are told is the God of Nature who gives
birth to panic, nightmares, is the inventor of masturbation, and a
rapist. As James Hillman has defined the archetype,

> Pan's world is in a continual state of subliminal panic just as it is
> in a continual state of subliminal sexual excitation. As the world
> is made by Eros, held together by the cosmogonic force and
> charged with the libidinal desire that is Pan . . . so its other side,
> panic . . . belongs to the same constellation.[78]

As for Dionysus, Plutarch informs us that the Egyptians also
represented Osiris as ithyphallic and that he was the same God as
the Bacchus (Dionysus) of Greek mythology along with the God
Eros of Orpheus.[79] The emblem of this God's celebration were "a
wine jar, a vine, a goat, a basket of figs, and then the phallus."[80]
We also know that a large phallus was displayed in the processions
held in honor of the God at Delos and that every Greek colony
regularly forwarded a phallus to the Athenian temple.

Hermes is the God of the underworld, he who leads us into the darkness of ourselves, pointing the path out; Pan is the God of Nature, of the primordial root of our instinctual lives; he rapes the naive psyche out of innocence, he is the masturbator; Dionysus, revealed to us in myth as a bisexual figure, is God of intoxication, liberator of our passions, the god of our darkness. All three of these Gods *are* the phallus. All three compose the figure of our Shiva in the West.

One other thing to consider is the fact that the serpent in the West is masculine. Alexander the Great was believed to have been the son of a serpent, as was Augustus.[81] The serpent of Eden was masculine, as are the snakes of the divine healer Asklepios. This latter figure was himself thought of as having sexual union with barren women in his snake form.[82] All of this is important in light of the fact that the constant companion of Athena was a snake,[83] and that the guardian demon of the Akropolis at Athens was the male serpent Erechtheus. An enormous statue of the Goddess with this serpent companion once stood on the Akropolis.[84] Therefore Athena and the masculine serpent are intimately connected in the same manner that Shiva is connected with Shakti in serpent form. The location of the ajna chakra in our Western version of the Kundalini system contains three phallic gods who represent the total function of Super-shiva. But what really ties this imagining up for me is the fact that one of these phallic gods was also given birth to by Zeus out of his own body — Dionysus. Whereas Athena was born from his head, Dionysus was born from his thigh: the masculine in the lower zone, the feminine in the higher, as Jung has suggested. By virtue of the fact that the two were born out of the body of their father, Dionysus and Athena may be thought of as brother and sister, as were Shiva and Shakti. And they represent a dichotomy: the sister symbolizes clarity and reflection, the brother ecstasy and freedom from reflection. Two sides of the same coin one might say.

Because I had been privileged to see a number of dreams by women in which the Kundalini presented itself as masculine, I was at first tempted to say that the masculine Kundalini was a phenomenon of feminine psychology alone. In the light of the above, however, I now strongly feel that the masculinity of the Kundalini applies to male psychology as well. The symbolism of the ensnared feminine is a collective problem shared by both men and women alike. All of this leads us to consider that we are today faced not only with the freeing of the feminine, but the resurrection of another kind of masculinity. Where anima is, animus is; any change in the nature of the one brings about a complementary change in the other. The portrayal of the masculine as that which is pure, solar, up there, unemotional, dry, and rational, always on target does not completely fit what we know about men. Obviously, during the creation of our Western model of masculinity a lot was left out. What was left out was the dark, emotional, instinctual, street-wise consciousness of Hermes, Pan, and especially Dionysus.

Whereas the myths we referred to earlier depicted a masculine deity removed from the plight of the feminine, stationary and fixed, the fluid and passionate nature of Dionysus, the fact that he changes easily from one form to another and that he is specifically a god of the feminine, suggests another way out of the dilemma of an ego-consciousness too far removed from the soul. In much of the same way that the appearance of the cult of Dionysus in Greek culture signalled the independence of women from the Demeter-like role of mother, wife, sister to man, so too may the arrival of a Dionystic stance on the shore of our psychic awareness free anima from earth, release Athena from Daddy.

James Hillman had alerted us to the idea that the way "to another consciousness thus begins by taking back those feminine aspects of the primal union, by returning to our own primary bisexuality."[85] By accepting the feminine, by doing more than observing her plight from the height of our intellectual note-taking and head-shaking, and by recognizing that the physiological qualities we have deemed inferior are actually projections of our own psychological interiority, we can restore our path to the androgyne.[86]

The mere conscious acceptance of the anima as idea however will not be enough. The activation of the androgyne calls for a fusion, a mingling of opposites into one permanent body. And this cannot be done without the freeing of anima first through a ritual immersion in anima, through methods that free up the waters of our imagination. Whether this will indeed lead to the creation of a yoga is to be seen.

My reflections have concerned themselves with what is eternal in all of us, the soul of our humanity without which the androgyne is a fiction.

NOTES

[1]"It is a remarkable fact that perhaps the majority of cosmogonic gods are of a bisexual nature. The hermaphrodite means nothing less than a union of the strongest and most striking opposites. In the first place this union refers back to a primitive state of mind, a twilight where differences and contrasts were either barely separated or completely merged. With increasing clarity of consciousness, however, the opposites draw more and more distinctly and irreconcilably apart." *Essays on a Science of Mythology*, C. G. Jung and C. Kerenyi, Harper Torchbooks, New York, 1963, p. 92.

[2]C. G. Jung, *CW* 9 (i) par. 512.

[3]"The splitting of the Original Man into husband and wife expresses an act of nascent consciousness; it gives birth to a pair of opposites, thereby making consciousness possible." Jung, *CW* 9 (ii), para. 320. Also see Maria von Franz, *Creation Myths*, Spring Publications, second unrevised printing, New York/Zurich, p. 155.

[4]Jung, *CW* 13, par. 456.

[5]"Mercurius is likened to the 'matrimonium' or coniunctio; that is to say he *is* the marriage on account of his androgynous form." Jung, *CW* 14, par. 12, p. 17.

[6]C. G. Jung: *Letters*, Gerhard Adler/Aniela Jaffe, editors, Princeton University Press, Princeton, New Jersey, 1975, vol. II, p. 394.

[7]Jung, *CW* 9 (i), par. 519.

[8]"The roles which Jung . . . assigns to the anima . . . all appear frequently and validly in the psychology of women. Anima phenomenology is not restricted to the male sex. . . The intensifications, exaggerations, and mythologizings that belong to the description of the anima do appear in women and may not be ascribed to her unconscious feminine personality, the woman within, or attributed to a minority of female genes." "Anima" by James Hillman, *Spring 1973*, Spring Publications, New York, p. 115.

[9]*ibid.*, pp. 114ff.

[10]cf. note 4 above and *Letters*, vol. II, *op. cit.*, p. 395.

[11]Jung, *CW*, 11, par. 268.

[12]Jung, *CW*, 8, par. 439.

[13]*ibid.*, par. 964. Also see, C. G. *Jung: Letters*, Princeton University Press, Princeton, N.J., 1973, vol. I, p. 433.

[14]"Synchronicity therefore means the simultaneous concurrence of a certain psychic state with one or more external events which appear as meaningful parallels to the momentary subjective state—and, in certain cases, vice versa." Jung, *CW*, 8, par. 850. Also, "certain phenomena of simultaneity or synchronicity seem to be bound up with the archetypes." *ibid.*, par. 841.

[15]"*Mundus Imaginalis* or the Imaginary and the Imaginal," by Henry Corbin, in *Spring 1972*, Analytical Psychology Club of New York, p. 10. Corbin's elucidation of the spiritual world of the Sufi corresponds with Jung's in that he too thought of the archetypes as existing independently of one another while at the same time being contained in one another. cf. *CW* 11, par. 440; also von Franz, *op. cit.* Lecture I, p. 10.

[16]Thus, the "work" on the androgyne demands the altruistic attitude of the early alchemist: "For the alchemist, the one primarily in need of redemption is not man, but the deity who is lost and sleeping in matter. Only as a secondary consideration does he hope that some benefit may accrue to himself from the transformed substance as the panacea, the *medicina catholica*. . . His attention is not directed to his own salvation through God's grace, but to the liberation of God from the darkness of matter. By applying himself to this miraculous work he benefits from its salutary effect, but only incidentally. He may approach the work as one in need of salvation, but he knows that his salvation depends on the success of the work, on whether he can free the divine soul." Jung, *CW* 12 (second edition, 1968), par. 420.

[17]*The Logos of the Soul*, Evangelos Christou, Dunquin Press, Vienna/Zurich, 1963, p. 102.

[18]*The Varieties of Religious Experience*, William James, Longmans, Green and Co., New York, 1910, p. 388.

¹⁹*ibid.*, p. 516.

²⁰"Therefore they determined the tao of heaven and called it the dark and the light. They determined the tao of the earth and called it the yielding and the firm. They determined the tao of man and called it love and rectitude." *The I Ching or Book of Changes*, Wilhelm/Baynes, trans., Princeton University Press, third edition, 1973, p. 264.

²¹"As opposites never unite at their own level . . . a supraordinate 'Third' is always required, in which the two parts can come together." Jung, *CW*, 9 (ii), par. 280.

²²*Creative Imagination in the Sufism of Ibn'Arabi*, Henry Corbin, Princeton University Press, Princeton, N.J., 1969, p. 80. Jung expressed this idea early in his career: "This aim of totality can be recognized neither by the science, whose end is in itself, nor by feeling, which lacks the faculty of vision belonging to thought. The one must lend itself as auxillary to the other, yet the contrast between them is so great that we need a bridge. This bridge is already given us in creative phantasy." *Psychological Types*, C. G. Jung, Harcourt, Brace & Co., Inc., New York, 1923, p. 77.
The transformative power of phantasy, later called active imagination, was a powerful issue in Jung's mind, *vide*: "All the difficulties you overcome in such a fantasy are symbolic expressions of psychological difficulties in yourself, and inasmuch as you overcome them in your imagination you also overcome them in your psyche." *Letters*, vol. I, *op. cit.*, p. 109.

²³Jung, *CW* 11, par. 889.

²⁵*Kama-Kala-Vilasa*, Sir John Woodroffe, trans., Ganesh & Co., Madras, third edition, 1961, p. 6.

²⁵"Thou are neither girl, nor maid, nor old. Indeed, thou are neither female nor male, nor neuter. Thou art inconceivable, immeasurable Power, the Being of all which exists, void of all duality, the Supreme Brahman, attainable in Illumination alone." From the *Mahakala-Samhita*, quoted in *S'akti and S'akta*, by Sir John Woodroffe, Ganesh & Co., Madras, sixth edition, 1965, p. 28.

²⁶*ibid.*, p. 39.

²⁷*The Serpent Power*, Sir John Woodroffe, Ganesh & Co., Madras, seventh edition, 1964, p. 41.

[28]*Introduction to Tantra Shastra*, Sir John Woodruffe, Ganesh & Co., Madras, second edition, 1952, p. 34.

[29]Briefly described, the system of the chakras in the human body is as follows:

The first chakra, *Muladhara* ("the root base"), is located midway between the genitals above and the anus below. Each chakra is given the image of the lotus, and the color of this lotus is crimson. It is square and its element is earth. It is here that the Kundalini in the form of a serpent coiled three times around the Divine Lingam or phallus, slumbers. This latter scene is found in the middle of a yellow triangle identified as the Yoni, or female genitals.

The second chakra, *Svadhisthana* (abode of Shakti), is located at the root of the genitals and within the *Susumna nadi*. The *nadi* is a channel, of which there are three. The *Susumna nadi* goes straight up the center of the spine. The *Ida nadi* is situated to the left of this *nadi* and the *Pingala nadi* is situated to the right. These two latter channels intertwine the central channel, both of them originating in the first chakra and both meeting in the fifth (ajna) chakra. The *Ida nadi* culminates in the left nostril, the *Pingala* in the right. The *Ida* is also known as the moon, the *Pingala* as the sun. This second chakra is the first to be located within the central channel. The first (Muladhara) is imagined as immediately at the base of the Susumna, the mouth of the slumbering Kundalini engulfing its base. The color of this lotus is vermilion and its element is water.

The third chakra, *Manipura* ("the city of the lustrous gem"), is located in the navel region. Its color is blue and its element is fire.

The fourth chakra, *Anahata* ("the sound which comes without the striking of any two things together"), is located at the level of the heart. Its color is ruddy and its element is air.

The fifth chakra, *Visuddha* ("completely purified"), is located at the base of the throat. Its color is a smoky purple and its element is ether.

The sixth chakra, *Ajna* ("Lotus of Command"), is located between the two eye-brows. Its color is white and it is imagined as existing beyond the zones of the five elements.

Above this last chakra is *Sahasrara* ("the lotus of a thousand petals"), in which Para-siva awaits the return of and conjunction with his Shakti, Kundalini.

The first three chakras (*Muladhara, Svadhisthana,* and *Manipura*) comprise the gross body, the last three the subtle.

The description of the chakras has been culled from *Kundalini Yoga* by M. P. Pandit, Ganesh & Co., Madras, second edition, 1962, p. 32ff. The translation of the chakra titles are from Heinrich Zimmer's "The Chakras of Kundalini Yoga," in *Spring 1975*, pp. 33ff.

³⁰cf. *The Serpent Power, op. cit.*, p. 228.

³¹The danger is that the aroused serpent-power might enter either the ida or the pingala, the result of which is disastrous. For a gruelling account of such a mishap I refer the reader to *Kundalini: The Evolutionary Energy in Man*, Gopi Krishna, Shambhala, Berkeley, 1971. Also see "On the Significance of the Indian Tantric Yoga," by Heinrich Zimmer, *Spiritual Disciplines*, edited by Joseph Campbell, Pantheon Books, New York, 1960.

³²*The Yoga Upanishad*, T. R. Srinivasa Ayyangar, trans., The Adyar Library, Madras, 1952.

³³cf. *The Serpent Power, op. cit.*, pp. 31ff.

³⁴ Jung, *CW, 8, par. 246.*

³⁵*ibid.*, par. 243.

³⁶Here, and in the greater portion of references to Jung's statements concerning the anima as the archetype of reflection and consciousness, I am indebted to James Hillman's research contained in his "Anima," (I & II), *Spring 1973, Spring 1974.*

³⁷Jung, *CW*, 11, par. 240, quoted in Hillman, *ibid.*, 1973, p. 125.

³⁸*ibid.*

³⁹*ibid.*, pp. 125-6.

⁴⁰*ibid.*, p. 126.

⁴¹cf. *Kundalini Yoga, op. cit.*, pp. 40ff.

⁴²Jung, *CW* 14, par. 129.

⁴³Jung, *CW* 11, par. 252.

⁴⁴*Gnosticism and Early Christianity*, Robert M. Grant, Harper Torchbooks, New York, 1966, pp. 19ff.

⁴⁵*ibid.* pp. 76, 77.

⁴⁶Jung, *CW*, 13, par. 454.

[47]*ibid.*, par. 457.

[48]*ibid.*, par. 455.

[49]Jung's ideas on the muladhara and svadhisthana chakras are culled from Lectures I & II of his "Psychological Commentary on Kundalini Yoga," published in *Spring 1975*.

[50]*ibid.* p. 11.

[51]*ibid.*, p. 15.

[52]*ibid.*, p. 9.

[53]". . . we begin in our conscious world, so our *muladhara* might be, not down below in the belly, but up in the head. . . In the East the unconscious is above, while with us it is below, so we can reverse the whole thing, as if we were coming down from *muladhara*, as if that were the highest centre." *ibid.*, p. 12.

[54]I must now alert the reader that I take leave of Jung's commentary on the Kundalini, becoming fully responsible for what follows.

[55]*The Discovery of the Unconscious*, Henri F. Ellenberger, Basic Books, New York, 1970, pp. 518ff.

[56]". . . mental productions are regularly present in all the psychoneuroses . . . and these . . . phantasies have important connections with the causes of the neurotic symptoms." "Hysterical Phantasies and their Relations to Bisexuality," in *Sigmund Freud: Collected Papers*, Basic Books, New York, 1959, vol. II, p. 51.

[57]*ibid.*, p. 53.

[58]*ibid.*, p. 57. While Freud makes this statement solely in relation to the symptoms of hysteria, his opening argument that all neurotic symptoms display phantasy production generalizes his observation.

[59]"The Theory of the Instincts," in *An Outline of Psychoanalysis*, Clara Thompson, editor, Modern Library, New York, 1955, p. 6.

[60]*ibid.*, p. 7.

[61]*ibid.*, p. 6.

[62]*ibid.*, p. 8.

[63]*ibid.*

[64]"The Development of the Sexual Function," *ibid.*, pp. 9-13.

[65]*ibid.*, p. 11.

[66]I am indebted here to Dr. James Hillman's *The Myth of Analysis*, Northwestern University Press, Evanston, Ill., 1972, p. 242, for bringing this information to my attention.

[67]"Whenever a psychological theory is forcibly applied, we have reason to suspect an archetypal fantasy-image is trying to distort reality . . ." Jung, *CW*, 9 (i), p. 69n.

[68]*The Sacred and the Profane: The Nature of Religion*, Mircea Eliade, Harcourt, Brace & World, New York, 1959, p. 13.

[69]"The spiritual development of the West has been along entirely different lines from that of the East and has therefore produced conditions which are the most unfavorable soil one can think of for the application of yoga." Jung, *CW*, 11, par. 876. Also see, "The Realities of Practical Psychotherapy," *CW*, 16, second edition.

[70]Jung, *CW*, 11, par. 876, 873.

[71]cf. *Freud and the Post-Freudians*, J. A. C. Brown, Penguin Books, Baltimore, 1961, p. 29.

[72]cf. Hillman, "Anima" (I), *op. cit.*, p. 117: "The *per definitionem* absence of anima in women is a deprivation of a cosmic principle with no less consequence in the practice of analytical psychology than has been the theory of penis deprivation in the practice of psychoanalysis."

[73]*The Homeric Gods*, Walter F. Otto, Beacon Press, Boston, 1954, p. 53.

[74]Adapted from Zimmer's recounting of the tale in *Myths and Symbols in Indian Art and Civilization*, Heinrich Zimmer, Harper Torchbooks, New YHork, 1962, pp. 128ff.

[75]*ibid.*, p. 129.

[76]*ibid.*, p. 127.

⁷⁷OTTO, *op. cit.*, p. 104.

⁷⁸*Pan and the Nightmare: Two Essays*, Wilhelm Heinrich Roscher, James Hillman, Spring Publications, Zurich, Switzerland, 1972, pp. xxvii.

⁷⁹*Sexual Symbolism: A History of Phallic Worship*, Richard Payne Knight, Thomas Wright, Bell Publishing Co., New York, reprint, mcmlvii, p. 29.

⁸⁰*Dionysus: Myth and Cult*, Walter F. Otto, Indiana University Press, Bloomington and London, 1955, p. 164.

⁸¹*Ancient Incubation Theory and Modern Psychotherapy*, C. A. Meier, Northwestern University Press, Evanston, Ill., 1967, p. 65.

⁸²*ibid.*, p. 63.

⁸³*The Greeks and their Gods*, W. K. C. Guthrie, Beacon Press, Boston, fourth printing, 1962, pp. 106ff.

⁸⁴*The Meridian Handbook of Classical Mythology*, Edward Tripp, Meridian, New York, 1970, p. 118.

⁸⁵*The Myth of Analysis*, James Hillman, Northwestern University Press, Evanston, Ill, 1972, p. 282.

⁸⁶"The *physiological* qualities which have been declared inferior and to belong to the female would now become *psychological* qualities appropriate to man or woman. Inferiority would no longer be only feminine, because we now see it as part of a conjoined human consciousness; and the feminine would no longer be inferior, because it belongs to this structure of generally human consciousness." *ibid.*, p. 282.

THE ALCHEMICAL LIGHT

The alchemists believed that nature contained an illuminating principle reminiscent of the soul's power concealed within the elementary world stuff. Because individuals were also thought of as composed of this stuff, it was expected that this luminary could be found within them as well. The light, according to their belief, was the archetypal principle that preceded all things and could be experienced by a turning about within.[1] Thomas Vaughan, admittedly elusive about the matter, wrote:

> The almighty God placed in the heart of the world, namely, in the earth—as He did in the heart of every other creature—a fire-life, which Paracelsus calls the Archaeus and Sendivogius the Central Sun . . . Over this Archaeus or central fire God hath placed His heaven, the sun and stars, He hath placed the head and the eyes over the heart. For between man and the world there is no small accord, and he that knows not the one cannot know the other.[2]

The Paracelsian term Archaeus is defined by Ruland as, "a most high, exalted, and invisible spirit, which is separated from bodies, is exalted and ascends; it is the occult virtue of Nature, universal in all things, the artificer, the healer."[3] According to Vaughan, Archaeus is the central sun contained within the heart of every creature and takes the shape of an invisible spirit that is the active principle in Nature. Ruland further identifies this spirit with another Paracelsian term, Adech:

> Adech is our interior and invisible man, who raises up in our minds the images or archetypes of all other things which our visible and exterior man copies and forms with his hands. Each works after his own nature, the invisible things unseen, the sensible, under form sensible, those things which are within the domain of the senses.[4]

The Archaeus and Adech have up to this point been described as a central and invisible sun that creates images which are then transformed into concrete realities. It is in this sense an independent creative principle that gives shape and form to the phenomenal world through the agency of the human mind. We come closer to understanding exactly what this principle is when we read Paracelsus' comments on Hermetic Astronomy and discover that the stars of heaven would not be able to affect us if not for the existence of a star within us that acts as a medium between the heavenly powers and our bodies. "There is one star that governs all things . . . its office is to operate in man . . . to turn and to change their senses and their minds . . . This same medium is and must be a star situated in those things where the supreme operates. By this medium is produced an effect on the substance and on the body."[5] This star in persons is imagination,[6] and in that it is described as a complete sun, the illuminating principle in nature.

The star composed of imagination is called a spirit, and, to the alchemical mind, the spirit is that thing which unites the soul with the body:

> The Spirit produces the Soul from the Body, and returns it when it is white. Therefore it is called the Life of the Soul—*Vita Animae.* Should the Spirit depart from the Soul it could not give the life. The Soul unites and conjoins the married, Body and Spirit; so the Spirit unites the Soul with the Body, so that it is all one thing.

Therefore, the medium connecting body to psyche is imagination. Paracelsus says as much:

The Archaeus is of a magnetic nature, and attracts or repulses other sympathetic or anti-pathetic forces belonging to the same plane . . . The vital force is not enclosed in man, but radiates around him like a luminous sphere, and it may be made to act at a distance. In those semi-material rays the imagination of man may produce healthy or morbid effects. It may poison the essence of life and cause diseases, or it may purify it after it has been made impure, and restore the health.[8]

Thus, the image is a power capable of affecting the human body. We are familiar with the idea of an image affecting the psychological well-being of an individual—such as the poor self-image handed down from a parent to a child that causes a stunting of his or her psychological growth. But Paracelsus implies more than this when he states that the image can directly affect the body. The depth psychologist, R. A. Lockhart expresses this involvement as follows:

. . . bodily organs and processes have the capacity to stimulate the production of psychic images, meaningfully related to the type of physical disturbances and its location.

Paracelsus believed that the image is capable of healing what it has poisoned, and Lockhart reports a case in which a man dying from widespread cancer had a series of dreams so profound that they caused a deep transformation of his personality to occur, after which time his cancer regressed. All of this gives some validity to the alchemists' claim that alchemy is capable of freeing the body from every form of suffering through work on the soul.[10] I do not mean to imply here that the alchemists created a material or chemical substance capable of freeing the body from its infirmities, but rather that the object of alchemy was to bring an individual into a proper and harmonious relationship between psyche and soma. Religious, mystical, and metaphysical considerations aside, if the techniques the alchemists employed did this and nothing more our high valuation of alchemy would be more than warranted. We must allow the possibility that "the medicine of the body is the image of the medicine of the soul, just as the infirmities of the soul are the image of the infirmities of the body,"[11] for such equations lead us toward where body and psyche unite and affect one another.

Commenting upon the importance of uniting feeling and intellect, Jung wrote: "The one must lend itself as auxiliary to the other yet the contrast between them is so great that we need a bridge. This bridge is already given us in creative phantasy. It is not born of either, for it is the mother of both."[12] For the alchemists, he tells us this bridge led to "an intermediate realm between mind and matter, i.e. a psychic realm of subtle bodies whose characteristic it is to manifest themselves in a mental as well as a material form."[13] Plato was aware of the reality and efficacy of this imaginal bridge when he wrote that there is an art capable of turning the soul away from the outer forms of the world toward the inner, and that this conversion of the soul is not one producing vision, but rather one bringing about its proper use of vision. In short, he anticipates Henry Corbin's suggestion that imagination is a trans-sensory organ of perception: " . . . this organ of knowledge must be turned around from the world of becoming together with the entire soul . . . until the soul is able to endure the contemplation of essence and the brightest region of being."[14] Apparently the uniting factor between body and psyche, between the outer heaven and the inner heaven, is the medium of imagination. This medium of imagination, the imaginal, is another space, a nowhere that in some way nonetheless meshes with our everyday reality. This may suggest to some that imagination is little more than fancy or phantasy. But what has been evoked is the matter of *work*, of the need to exert an effort of will that essentially calls for an inversion of selfhood, a giving up of self. This demand alerts us to the fact that the initial movement in the direction of imagination was a strict regime of prayer and monastic discipline.

Prayer in this stage was more likely a petition for aid[15] which in time gave way to a mode of contemplation whose emphasis was that of establishing an inner dialogue. As William James put it, prayer "or inner communion with the spirit thereof—be that spirit 'God' or 'law'—is a process wherein work is really done, and spiritual energy flows in and produces effects, psychological or material within the phenomenal world."[16] It is at exactly this point that imagination enters the picture.

Imagination does not merely refer us to a pleasant passage of images across the screen of our consciousness, but a visual dialogue that engages the energies of our psyche to the same degree that it becomes engaged with the phenomenal world. This dialogue serves not only to act as a bridge to the imaginal, but to give it its place as the other half of what we would call our wholeness. This was the great discovery of alchemy: that we can take an active part in the on-going creation of Genesis through the medium of imagination. If the image gives birth to psychic life, and psychic life in turn manufactures the material person-made world from the ideas clustered around the image, then the fullness of life is to be found in an active participation with the image at its own level as well. Whether one wishes to call such an involvement meditation, contemplation, imaging, or prayer—it is a participation in otherness, in the undefinable ground of life.

This is what is referred to in the *Hermetica* when we are told that, prior to being in the world, soul and mind had been Life and Light, and that only those who are capable of recollecting this will "learn to know that you are made of them, . . . [and] go back into Life and Light."[17] All of this is another way of saying that the image, and imagination, is life. If one can imagine living a day without the experience of those images that normally pass through one's mind, this seemingly metaphysical statement will take on a different and quite concrete meaning. Without even the basic experience of mental images needed to recall where we parked our cars, left our hats, first met a person we have met again, there would be little to us. The philosophic and Hermetic traditions take this one step further: we are essentially dead, prisoners in Plato's cave, as long as we do not engage in the imaginal life that has given birth to our psyches in the first place. "Image and meaning are identical,"[18] so the degree to which we give emotional validity to the image is equal to the meaning we are capable of discovering in the life that the image creates.

But the process is not without its dangers, for what we are speaking of here is the petitioning of a dimension capable of shattering all that we identify with consciousness. The alchemical demand of sealing the vessel refers us to the importance of keeping this experience in some way separate and distinct from our everyday existence. One might say that it is overlapping of these two dimensions that turns the mystical or transformative into the pathological. The alchemical vessel, or rather its employment in a symbolic sense, was a way by which the impersonal reality of the soul—which could lead to a depersonalization experience of pathological proportions—could be kept from contaminating one's relationship to the world outside. Thus, we find a petitioner asking how one might arrive at the 'Supersensual Ground' without the destruction of his personality:

> How am I to wait for the rising of this glorious Sun, and how am I to seek in the Centre, this Fountain of Light, which may enlighten me throughout, and bring all my properties into perfect

Harmony? I am in Nature, as I said before; and which Way shall
I pass through Nature, and the Light thereof, so that I may come
into the Supernatural and Supersensual Ground, whence this true
Light, which is the Light of Minds, doth arise; and this *without
the Destruction of my Nature, or quenching the Light of it, which
is my Reason?*[19]

So we see that the alchemist and the mystic were well aware
of the necessity of keeping these two worlds separate and distinct.
It is apparent such observations were not spontaneous revelations
but the result of painstaking observation and experience. The stuff
of present-day psychology obviously had its beginnings with such
experiments centuries ago. The problem is that psychology does
not set out to define the imaginal, but rather the degree of our
pathological relationship to it. There is no geography of the soul
or spirit available for those who would wish to journey there. The
creation of such a geography obviously demands travellers who have
made the journey. The most we can do until their arrival is piece
out the descriptions left to us by those who have been centuries
before.

The opening stages of the journey demand purification, meditation, and the withdrawal of attention from material sensations up
to the point when

> the imaginative faculty will turn your thoughts to imagine and
> picture [mental contents] *as if* ascended in the higher worlds up
> the roots of his soul . . . until the imagined image reaches his
> highest source and there the images of the [supernal] lights are
> imprinted on his mind *as if* he imagined and saw them in the same
> way in which his imaginative faculty normally pictures in his mind
> mental contents deriving from the world . . . [20]

Here we arrive at the complicated issue of imaginal geography,
for whereas in the stage where the soul was to be pulled back from
'out there,' from the world of phenomena, it was assumed that its
withdrawal landed it 'in here,' in psyche. But no sooner is that
achieved when we are invariably presented with images of ascension. The difficulty has to do with the fact that, to our way of thinking today, 'up there' is associated with 'out there.' What we have
to be reminded of here is that the imaginal also describes itself in
terms of spatial co-ordinates; the famous alchemical dictum, 'that
which is below is as that which is above, and that which is above
is as that which is below," directs us to the placement of the im-

aginal world relative to ours. There is no reason we should not expect to find an above and below in the imaginal without reference to our spatial position in the phenomenal world.

And yet the experience of ascension and descension (as it transpires in the imaginal) expresses itself through our bodies—that is, through our sensory system, to give us the impression that it is happening 'out here.' That these imaginal happenings do cause the individual sometimes to believe that their expression is happening 'out there' is clearly shown in those Ecclesiastical depictions of saints and other mortals receiving an influx of spirit pouring down from the sky.

Such distinctions are important, for they help us separate the experience of the imaginal from the phenomenal without losing the quality of the experience, while at the same time safeguarding against a destructive inundation of the imaginal. As we should recall from our earlier pages, this was of major concern to those who wished to experience the 'Supersensual Ground' without the loss of their reason. It at the same time serves to 'locate' imaginal activity in much the manner that mythology locates gods and goddesses at a variety of geographical points on the earth. In the same way that a favorite spot in your garden might elicit memories of activities you had undertaken there, so too does locating co-ordinates within the imaginal allow recollective memory to become activated. For this reason alchemical treatises always abound in descriptions of Biblical or mythological places. Such landscapes serve as catalysts for the interior process.

Returning to the Safed Kabbalist Hayyad Vital's account of the soul's ascension, we are drawn even further into the geography of the imaginal. We should note in particular his statement that the meditator ascends towards the *roots* of his soul. The source of the image is Plato:

> As concerning the most sovereign form of soul in us we must conceive that heaven has given it to each man as a guiding genius—that part which we say dwells in the summit of our body and lifts us from earth towards our celestial affinity, like a plant whose roots are not in earth, but in the heavens. And this is most true, for it is to the heavens, whence the soul first came to birth, that the divine part attaches the head or root of us and keeps the whole body upright.[21]

As our account from the *Gloria Mundi* clearly shows, this same image was taken over by the alchemists: "Man may be compared to an inverted tree: for he has his roots or his hair in the air, while other trees have their hairs, or their roots, in the earth, and as the Sages say, . . . the root of their minerals is in the air, and their head in the earth."[22]

Whereas in Kabbalistic accounts the roots of the soul contain the supernal lights, or the sefiroth, in the *Hermetica*[23] we are told that the ascending soul must pass through the planetary zones in order to be stripped of the dark qualities originally assigned to it by each planet. This idea is implied in our passage from the *Gloria Mundi*, for the minerals contained in the roots of the inverted tree-soul refer us to the planets whose attributes they symbolize. In each instance, therefore, a journey must be undertaken through the planetary zones, or what Plato refers to as "those circuits in the head that were deranged at birth."[24] These references are particularly important when we recall that the alchemists thought of the planets as contained within us: "For it is true that the external stars affect the man, and the internal stars in man effect outward things, in fact and in operation, the one on the other."[25]

We inherit a two-fold image: the alchemist and the philosopher draw the nourishment for their souls from the imaginal, where the roots of their souls are planted. This is accomplished through imagination which allows the alchemist to journey to each mineral contained in the tree's branches in an attempt to turn each to gold.

With these few references to philosophy and alchemy we can now easily discern the meaning of the imagery offered us in the following excerpt:

> If any one were to take common metallic gold and silver, and tried to resolve those metals into mercury, he would be doing a very foolish thing. It is a result that cannot be brought about by any chemical process . . . But these sages did not speak of common gold and silver, which must always remain what they are, and can never become anything else, and certainly cannot aid the development of other metals . . . No, the *living* fruit (the real living gold and silver) we must seek *on the tree*, for only there can it grow, and increase in size, according to the possibilities of its nature. This tree we must transplant . . . into a better and richer soil, and to a sunnier spot . . . I wish you to understand that Mercury, which is a most excellent tree . . . must be taken and transplanted into a soil that is near to the Sun . . . —in the garden of the Sages, the *Sun* sheds its genial influence day and night . . .

> There our *tree* is watered with the rarest dew, and the fruit which
> hangs upon the trees swells and ripens and expands.[26]

Our writer begins by stating flatly that the gold and silver to
be created are not the common gold and silver but a living fruit
to be found upon a tree identified as Mercury, the spirit *par excellence* of alchemy whose identification with flowing and reflective quicksilver easily brings to mind the idea of imagination—
that which flows and reflects images. This tree must be uprooted
from the barren soil of the commonplace activity of imagination
and replanted in the garden of philosophy. There in the garden,
true gold and silver may be cultivated.

Imagination is spirit; in some of our selections it is referred to
directly as such. The reflective and fluviant quality of the Spirit
Mercurius in its alchemical depiction as quicksilver aptly symbolizes
the activity of imagination: it flows, it fragments, it reflects. But
we could just as easily bring alchemical material to bear on the idea
that the soul is imagination, thus reminding us of the alchemists'
statement that "Also the Soul is called Spirit, and the Spirit is called
Soul."

Jung tells us that there are five instincts: hunger, sexuality, drive
to activity, reflection, and creativity. The first three are easily understandable and need no explanation. Reflection "is the cultural instinct *par excellence,* and its strength is shown in the power of culture
to maintain itself in the face of untamed nature,"[27] in its ability to
interfere with stimuli whose tendency is to trigger instinctive discharges. Whereas in other creatures a stimulus is followed by an
impulse to act that immediately discharges itself into the world, this
'specifically human'[28] instinct carries the impulse over to a psychic
realm where it is either held in check or dissipated. The charge that
would normally move outward into this world becomes turned inward, toward the psyche where it becomes the object of reflection
in the form of images.[29]

From what Jung has said, we might surmise that there occurs
a radical alteration of impulse from what might be thought of as
instinctual concreteness (making real the impulse) to a state of
psychic immateriality, or a transformation of the concrete into image. Jung describes this latter process as psychization, but the mystics
would have and did call it death. In Jung we find, "In spite or perhaps
because of its affinity with instinct, the archetype represents the
authentic element of spirit, but a spirit which is not to be identified
with the human intellect, since it is the latter's *spiritus rector.*"[30]

So psychization might be thought of as spiritualization:

> Psychic processes therefore behave like a scale along which con-
> sciousness "slides." At one moment it finds itself in the vicinity
> of instinct, and falls under its influence; at another, it slides along
> to the other end where spirit predominates and even assimilates
> the instinctual processes most opposed to it.[31]

The alchemical and mystical demand that the gates of the senses
be closed (and the soul recalled from its materialistic involvement
with the world) directs us to this psychological process of reflection. The 'death' of an instinctual response and its psychization,
a process in which the response becomes image, is in direct cor-
relation to the retrieval of the soul for the purpose of its ascension
up the contemplative ladder of imagination as described by the Kabbalist Vital several pages back. It also fully answers the description of the alchemical nigredo in which the body dies and the soul
ascends.

Another way of putting it is that the plane of imagination is
created by death—it is the death of the soul's bodily impulse that
turns it into image and thus subject to spirit. Remembering that imagination has been spoken of as illumination and as a brightness
by the alchemists, it is not without interest that in Plato the pure
soul is compared to light,[32] and that the place where all souls go
to in death, Hades, is described like the soul: "glorious, pure, and
invisible."[33] Thus, Soul and Spirit are not only connected by death,
but by imagination. In fact, the implication is that without the interplay of soul and spirit there would be no imagination. Imagination
might be compared to the *idea* of a mirror whose existence could
not come to pass without the silvering substance of mercury on the
one hand, and glass on the other. The combination of the two creates
a place of reflection. Thus, the combination, the reflection and
clarity, of soul and spirit create imagination.

We have given indications that the alchemical process heavily
relied upon methods that called for an immersion in imaginal processes. We have also indicated that these processes lie far beneath
the threshold of what we normally identify as consciousness, and
that because of their foreign nature to the twentieth century mind
they often burst upon us in a manner not to excite as much as to
terrorize and break down the boundaries of personality. It has also
been implied that such breakdowns of our ego defenses have often
been referred to as a prerequisite for any type of transformation

along the lines that mysticism and alchemy have laid down. Our difficulty today, therefore, is to be found in our attitude towards such intrusions of the imaginal. Textbooks warn us of pathology— and in many instances such intrusions properly answer that description. But the reason why this is the case has not so much to do with the events themselves as with the reception of the event. A psychology or religion that holds the imaginal at bay is bound to suffer at its hand. One cannot adapt a religious mode of being without at some point being forced to experience what one is talking about, nor can one admit that one is a psychological being without experiencing the fullness of one's psychology.

Religions and psychology, alchemy and mysticism, all deal with similar issues. The difference lies in the terminology and the ritual engagement. Whether one goes for guidance to a priest, a doctor, or one's dreams, they are in all instances deeply engaged with the nature of being. To deal with only those aspects that link us to the phenomenal world is to deny and ignore the deeper and far more personal issues of life and death. Alchemy is a tradition that found itself almost unwittingly attempting to incorporate these issues through the phenomenon of imagination. Admittedly, the method was not created out of a body of doctrinal beliefs. Each alchemist appears to have discovered the method for himself—and what he discovered was the operation of what he called Nature: a natural process in psyche. Whereas in the East this process was worked into a method such as yoga, here in the West it was allowed to develop with very little modification or restraint. In the East, when an incorrect employment of such methods would yield what we would call pathological phenomena, such phenomena were regarded as the outcome of wrong techniques—not as illness. Perhaps it is because we have no technique, no guiding rules for the experience of the imaginal, that these phenomena that historically produced mystical or religious doctrines, instead became the science of psychology. That is, because the experience of the imaginal had no containing ritual, no alchemical vessel, it came to be seen as a disturbance of persons rather than a disturbance of methodology. Therapy as we know it today may be nothing more than an attempt to compensate for the absence of a containing religion that would receive and portray these experiences as transformative rather than degenerative. This might explain the striking similarities to be found between certain aspects of mystical and pathological experiences, similarities suggesting that they are, in fact, the same experience.

As can be seen by what has gone before us, the tangle of ideas that form the body of alchemy have their source in a number of traditions that, at first sight, seem to have little to do with alchemy. That alchemy, however, has served as the receptacle for practically every type of speculation about the nature of the soul, spirit, and body indicates that in it we have a drawerful of imaginings about what is basic in being, whether or not we accept the poetry of the terms employed to define it. At the very least we have discovered that alchemy is a legitimate expression of a Western mystical tradition that appeared just before the emergence of the Scientific Revolution. At the most, we might discover that the alchemists were involved with a never-ending Genesis, an imaginal world without end.

NOTES

[1]"O Man, thou art with thy soul in the inward; but thy soul's will hath turned itself about with Adam into the outward; therefore, if thou wilt behold God and the Eternity, *turn* thyself about with thy will into the inward, and then thou art as God himself." *The Works of Jacob Behme*, William Law, tran., London, 1781.

[2]*The Works of Thomas Vaughan*, Arthur Edward Waite, editor, Theosophical Publishing House, London, 1919, p. 403.

[3]*A Lexicon of Alchemy*, Martin Ruland the Elder, Arthur Edward Waite, trans. and editor, John M. Watkins, London, 1964, p. 36.

[4]*ibid.*, p. 6.

[5]*The Hermetic and Alchemical Writings of Paracelsus*, Arthur Edward Waite, trans. and editor, two volumes, James Elliott & Co., London, 1967, vol. II, p. 285.

[6]"The imagination is the mouth of the body which is not visible. It is also the sun of man which acts within its own sphere after the manner of the celestial luminary. It irradiates the earth, which is man, just as the material sun shines upon the material world . . . And as the sun sends its force on a spot which it shines upon, so also the imagination, like a star, bursts upon the thing which it affects." *ibid.*, vol. II, p. 7.

[7]Ruland, *op. cit.*, p. 31.

⁸*Paracelsus: Life and Prophecies,* by Franz Hartmann, Rudolf Steiner Publications, Blauvelt, New York, 1973, p. 133.

⁹"Cancer in Myth and Dream," by R. A. Lockhart, *Spring* 1977, p. 10.

¹⁰"Our Art frees not only the body, but also the soul from the snares of servitude and bondage; it enobles the rich, and comforts and relieves the poor. Indeed, it may be said to supply every human want, and to provide a remedy for every form of suffering." *The New Pearl of Great Price,* Arthur Edward Waite, trans. and editor, Vincent Stuart, Ltd., London 1963, reprint of 1984 edition, p. 119.

¹¹*The Epistles of Ali Pul,* J. W. Hamilton-Jones, trans., John M. Watkins, London, 1951, p. 5.

¹²*Psychological Types,* by C. G. Jung, Harcourt, Brace & Company, Inc. New York/London, 1923, p. 77.

¹³*Collected Works of C. G. Jung,* Routledge & Kegan Paul, London, 1953, vol. 12, par. 395.

¹⁴"The Republic," in *The Collected Dialogues of Plato,* Edith Hamilton and Huntington Cairns, editors, Princeton University Press, 1973, Book vii, par. 518d.

¹⁵"Then fall upon thy knees, and with a humble and contrite heart render to Him the praise, honour, and glory due for the hearing of thy prayer, and ask Him again and again to continue to thee His grace, and to grant that, after attaining the full and perfect knowledge of this profound Mystery, thou mayest be enabled to use it to the glory and honour of His most Holy Name, and for the good of thy suffering fellow men." from "The Sophie Hydrolith," in *The Hermetic Museum,* Arthur Edward Waite, editor and trans. John Watkins, London, 1953, 2 vols., reprint of 1893 edition, vol. I, pp. 74-5.

¹⁶*The Varieties of Religious Experience,* by William James, Longmans, Green & Co., New York, 1910, page 389.

¹⁷*Hermetica,* Walter Scott, trans. in 4 volumes, Oxford, 1924, vol. I, p. 17 & 21.

¹⁸Jung, *CW,* 8 par. 402.

¹⁹Behme, *op. cit.,* vol. IV, P. 89, my italics.

[20]Hayyim Vital, quoted in *Joseph Karo: Lawyer & Mystic*, by R. J. Zwi Werblowsky, The Jewish Publication Society of America, Philadelphia, 1977, p. 69.

[21]"Timaeus," *Plato's Cosmology*, trans. by Francis Macdonald Cornford, Routledge & Kegan Paul, London/New York, 1971, 90a, p. 353.

[22]*Hermetic Museum, op. cit.*, vol. I, p. 218.

[23]"Timaeus," *op. cit.*, 90d, p. 354.

[25]*Hermetic & Alchemical Writings of paracelsus, op. cit.*, II, p. 285.

[26]*Hermetic Museum, op. cit.*, vol. I, pp. 144–5.

[27]Jung, *CW* 8, par. 243.

[28]*ibid.*, par. 241.

[29]*ibid.*, par. 242.

[30]*ibid.*, par. 406.

[31]*ibid.*, par. 408.

[32]"Republic," *op. cit.*, Book vii, 518.

[33]"Phaedo," *Collected Dialogues of Plato, op. cit.*, 80d.

ON THE POSSESSION
OF CONSCIOUSNESS

I
The Frame of Consciousness

"Psychology is concerned with the act of seeing and not with the construction of new religious truths."
C.G. Jung

At the very least, we can say that the term "consciousness" refers us to a state of sensory awareness, of simple presence vacillating between multiple levels and combinations of attention. But if one should be physically exhausted, ill, or in pain then the ability to summon and focus the requisite amount of energy necessary to maintain attention is considerably diminished. Even with all things being favorable, the energy necessary to negotiate the simple state of "being awake" or minimally conscious dissipates of its own accord little before half of our 24 hour day is over. It is upon this demanding somatic base that simple awareness and attention must and does construct and maintain its daily participation in being. The body that carries it dictates to consciousness, marking and testing its limits hour by hour.

In addition, the limitations of those sensory organs that gather data about the phenomenal world for us to interpret, seek meaning in and be moderately present to, leave us ignorant of awareness and information commonly accessible to our household pets. All of this suggests the existence of yet other phenomenal nuances, textures, hues, decibels and details, rich in their unavailability, foresting a world we are always *present to* but never fully *in.*

And of what is left us to attend, we must assiduously filter, screening the data relevant to our grasping the object of our attention with our attention. In short, the intensity of awareness we commonly identify as consciousness can only be achieved by purposefully limiting and narrowing our experience of the world. And finally, in our innate drive to discover a meaningful order or nomos in all things, we populate the empty spaces in our knowledge with the imagination of our memories, or the fabrications of our ignorance, thus filling what is unidentifiable by us with fancy parading as the truth of the thing—projecting upon the thing what we would have the thing be. In turn, the nomos so created must follow the guidelines of the socially defined reality that contains it, the larger or collective nomos. The dialectical process that occurs between these two meaningful orders constitutes a reality frame by which the individual is continually assured that things are as they should be.[1]

Reality frames are "given" to individuals as instruments of society's definition of reality. Such society—be it the society of my family, peers, or nation—always presumes that its frame correctly defines and delineates reality. Individuals readily align themselves with such frames, for by so doing they are assured inclusion in and protection by the community they seek agreement with. But more important, they help the individual in establishing a frontier of order against the tide of "unreason" promised by the unconscious. It is by the adjustment to existing reality frames, slowly developed throughout the life-cycle, that we create the thing called consciousness. But consciousness is a fragile and limited construction, the breakdown of which allows mental contents previously excluded to flow more freely into phenomenal awareness.[2] Such breakdowns usher in phenomena peculiar to altered states of consciousness, which each culture in turn classifies as being either specialized (religious, shamanistic, medical) or deviant (evil, possessed, pathological), i.e., social responses, different from the natural attitude but still under its jurisdiction.

It should be obvious that the construction of a reality demands that it be compact, manageable, and subject to little variation for easy maintenance. Thus, the omission of phenomena that are peripheral to the situation at hand, and the ensuing narrowing of attention, is essentially a strengthening of both consciousness and the frame within which it operates and is contained. But reality frames are delicate, subject to failure and breakdown by a variety of ostensibly simple phenomena. Extreme physical stress, whether induced by the religious regime of a yoga or by circumstance, inevitably leads to an alteration of consciousness. Sensory deprivation yields the same result, as do any number of other techniques designed to interrupt the facile operation of the frame by causing a "deautomatization of the psychological structures that organize, limit, select, and interpret perceptual stimuli."[3] Such an altered state always occurs when a reality frame is challenged. It is an old technique of those spiritual disciplines that seek to free the individual from one frame so that he might be initiated into a new and ideologically better reality. Such techniques lie at the heart of political brainwashing in the twentieth century. The breaking of the frame leads to a "breakdown" of the individual during which time a multitude of psychic phenomena can and often do manifest themselves. One lands in "an underlying realm of unreason which threatens . . . and envelops . . . all the forms of . . . natural existence . . . an area of unforeseeable freedom where frenzy is unchained."[4] Almost without exception the phenomena accompanying altered states of consciousness give rise to explanations and descriptions of states referred to as mystical, religious, numinous and other-worldly. Whether (or not) these experiences reveal the existence of a divine and transpersonal reality is not what concerns us here, but rather the fact that *where* such phenomena are found we can suspect the rupture of a reality frame immediately preceding their appearance. Because consciousness is a social phenomenon,[5] we shall have to consider its existence from at least a partially phenomenological viewpoint in order to grasp what the possession of consciousness *means* as a psychological state.

II
The Sociology of Consciousness

Like language, the social is an autonomous reality.
Claude Lévi-Strauss

Because "every individual is virtually an enemy of civilization,"[6] Freud held that in order for civilization to maintain and transmit knowledge, create regulations that would allow people to act in accord with one another (along with the complications inherent in the distribution of wealth), the individual must sacrifice certain instinctual responses for the purpose of maintaining the *status quo.*[7] Out of all this there arises the need for civilization to impose upon a resisting majority a reality created and enforced by a powerful and coercive minority. In that "there are present in all men destructive and therefore anti-social and anti-cultural trends," every civilization "must be built up on coercion and renunciation of instinct,"[8] for the "principal task of civilization, its actual *raison d'etre,* is to defend us against nature."[9] The penultimate defense displays itself in the manifestation of the super-ego "because in keeping with the course of human development . . . external coercion gradually becomes internalized . . . man's super-ego, takes it over and includes it amongst its commandments."[10] It is only in "those in whom it [the internalization of society's coerciveness] has taken place [who] are turned from being opponents of civilization into being its vehicles."[11] Finally, this coerciveness can be truly effective only "so long as it is feared."[12] In essence, Freud tells us that the construction and maintenance of social reality can occur only if the major portion of its participants have been coerced into dictated norms of being by the fear of punishment and retribution.

Peter Berger has outlined the dialectical process by which this program is effected, the internalization of external coercion Freud spoke of constituting the third step or stage in Berger's system.[13] However, whereas Freud demonstrated how individuals are brought in line with a *status quo* condition, Berger shows why society is by nature forced to proceed in such a manner. He explains that the society-building that is peculiar to humanity is based upon the fact that the human world is an open system, as opposed to the non-human world which is predestined by highly specialized and directed instincts and thereby contained and closed. Thus, the non-human world is a biologically determined reality in contrast to the human world which, while on the one hand sharing certain common features with the non-human world, also has at its disposal a certain quantum of independent will. At least this is one way to look at the situation. We might as easily surmise from this that the human world's openness reflects the outcome of a mutation that displays itself as a deficiency when compared with the non-human world. It is this that causes us, through objectivation, to create a reality that appears to be little effected by our actions. This is what Husserl referred to when he wrote that the world of the natural attitude, wherein, "strictly understood, what presents itself to the individual as 'real' should be taken as 'what is given,' not as that which is real."[14] In other words, what is given is the objectiviation of our externalizations, thereby causing us to forget that what we face in society is the projection of psychic structures shaped by our experience of society.

Thus, Freud's comments regarding the super-ego assuming the coercive task of society through internalization suggest that the thing we call consciousness (the object of all psychologies) has its origins in our own projections; that socially-created reality initially derives its form from the psyche, and that the internalization of this form then bears along with it the content peculiar to the society in which the individual lives.[15] This "content," composed of the mores, laws, beliefs, etc., then defines the parameters of the thing we call consciousness, giving rise to a reality-frame by which the individual defines his being-in-the-world. What we are watching here is an unconscious and spontaneous process of the psyche in its response to the phenomenal world. While society may at times willfully and purposefully coerce individuals into performance, it is as a rule unaware that it goes about its world-building in this manner—which is indeed the very essence of the natural attitude. That it does so is no small matter, for by failing to see what it does, it is inevitably forced to justify its action as one that is "for the good of the people," thereby legitimatizing unconscious power in both itself and in its citizens.

It follows that every theory of reality, and therefore every reality, produces a theory of personality, and that every such theory sets out how the ideal member of the group should behave. It is by such idealized figures that society measures its members. In the past, the guardians of this norm arrived at their authority by pointing to religious scripture. The definition of what was normal then (as now)

was always determined and modified by what was considered deviant or abnormal. The handbooks created to test for the presence
of witchcraft, magic, possession, etc. attest to this early need to
single out and correct those who did not abide by the norm. The
question asked was in principle: Does the individual conform to
the established reality frame of the group? While many still live by
the earlier forms of such reality-testing, psychology in the twentieth century has increasingly become the standard-bearer. It is the
psychologist to whom we now turn when we wish to discover what
is normal or abnormal behavior. We do so because we have been
taught that psychology not only tells us how personal reality should
be experienced, but also promises to return the individual to that
reality should his actions not conform with those of the norm. The
coercion Freud spoke of as a necessary device to align the individual
with society's needs here becomes a medical issue. But, contrary
to Szasz's well-known complaint[16] I would stress that this align-
ment correctly defines the purpose behind all schools of healing in
both the past and present. The role of the shaman, witch doctor,
and healer has always been one of returning the individual to an
established norm, of correcting that which has gone awry. Healing
by definition is corrective and restorative, and therefore coercive.
It convinces the individual that his return to the established reality-
frame is not only desirable but necessary, if not imperative. From
this one could say that the general public's recent and impassioned
involvement with folk and shamanistic traditions—along with the
metaphysic of healing supplied by such things as the laying on of
hands, guided imagery, the employment of crystals, prayers, man-
tras, channeling, and the multitude of therapies currently in favor—
is a social cry for answers to ontological questions it is normally
incumbent upon a society to supply and authoritatively so. That
such a state presently exists indicates that our culture is no longer
capable of offering a prescription that would satisfy all of the collective needs. In short, what we are present to is a breakdown of
our culture's reality frame.
    It is necessary to take note that the "fundamental coerciveness
of society lies not in its machineries of social control, but in its power
to constitute and to impose itself as reality."[17] In this manner do
both the societal roles and the institutions that foster them, the products of individuals collectively acting, take on an objective reality
cloaked with the illusion of eternality.[18] Long before the individual
enters the world the roles he or she will be expected to play—often

determined by the availability or absence of desirable social, racial, monetary, and geographic positions—are well defined. An attempt is then made to impose these roles upon individuals through the projection of idealized states fitting our socially prescribed condition and position. The institutions that define these roles, as other institutions, have further defined what is normal to their needs. The degree to which we accept these norms is the degree to which projections become contractual agreements. Such things do not happen to us, we agree to let them happen. The reality of these roles, in that they exist prior to our birth and the birth of our immediate ancestors, gives them an eternal flavor. In that their origins have long been forgotten, thus allowing their historicity to suggest eternality, we have come to assign them archetypal qualities—a Platonic *a priori* existence which only further serves to inculcate in us the obeisance Freud correctly observed was necessary for a culture to survive. By such prescriptions do we learn how a son, daughter, mother, father, wife, husband, should act and behave. We find assurance in this "shouldness" by pointing to the past, and all of those texts that have been produced to support this position. In such a manner do we find justification for all of our roles and institutions.[19]

Society goes to great expense to make these objectivations valued and honored realities, and therefore seeks to maintain them from generation to generation by initiating individuals into objectivated meanings at an early age. But these objectivations are not simply meanings, intellectual realizations the individual grasps and then performs—the individual literally becomes the meanings to the degree that he fulfills their definitions, sometimes becoming the living embodiment and model of objectivated meanings.[20] The continued success of a society is measured by its ability to maintain and transmit such traditions in this manner.

Once the world has been internalized and the individual takes on the archetypal role society says he must play, then he can access the meaning of the role through an act of introspection.[21] Because one's turn towards oneself for counsel is a willed event, the individual assumes that the counsel he seeks and receives is his own.[22] However, unless one has become capable of differentiating the internalized social proscriptions from the values one has personally constructed (which may or may not agree with society's values), the authority and numinosity of societal values will win over. Because societal and personal value systems do not necessarily coincide, we can expect tension and conflict to occur in any attempt to resolve the paradox. Obviously, it is far easier to either resolve or completely avoid such conflict by giving in to internalized societal directives. In short, a sacrifice must occur each time such a conflict is resolved in this manner. However, if the individual seeks to maintain his position and resolve the conflict, the tension between the two value systems imperils the fabric of the natural attitude offered up by societal prescription. It is at this juncture where the reality frame, composed of both societal and personal values, threatens to rupture, with all of the concomitant symptoms and results.

If the unconscious can in greater part be shaped by the internalization of society, then to the degree that we habitually concede our positions, what we turn towards in ourselves for wise counsel is not ourselves but others—the opinions of society. Thus, "my unconscious" is actually a collective unconscious composed of society's internalized injunctions. Jung said as much when he wrote that the "unconscious is, as the collective psyche, the psychological representative of society."[23] In that many introspections ostensibly call upon memories wherein we find "the lessons" of our interaction with society, our counsel is derived from social responses to our compliance with or deviation from the roles defined by the natural attitude.

It is obvious that the internalization of society does not guarantee total and continued socialization of the individual; that the personal values attained from experience will always come into conflict with the *status quo*. Subjected to a variety of personal experiences, the value system created by the individual would considerably diminish society's internalized hold. But because the major portion of any collective body fulfills the expectations of the natural attitude, and thereby meet the requirements of the norm, we can assume that society in some manner manages to compensate for and correct (if not restrict) the individual's personally created value system. The purpose of any number of institutions is to maintain the natural attitude—*religion, law, psychology, etc.*—and I would here also add the institution of the dream and dream interpretation as yet another social device guided toward this end.[24]

The deficiency in human society, the absence of pure meaning and knowing, is seemingly corrected in us when we are presented with a well-defined nomos, whatever the substance of that nomos is. Within that nomos those answers to the question of being that are of importance to us are given, and to the degree that we are true believers of the proposed nomos, we can relax in the best of all possible worlds. If something should go amiss, we are assured that this mishap has come about either because of preordination, or simply because we have not complied with the regulations of the nomos we embrace. All of this is another way of saying that participation in a nomos demands adherence to standards by which the individual may be known as "normal," this latter identification being the prerequisite for the sharing of social rights based upon the concept of equality. Those who fail the nomos are then considered deviant, abnormal and/or pathological.

From the above it should be clear that one does not truly have consciousness simply by virtue of being human and aware, but that, to the degree it is defined by the internalization of social reality, consciousness possesses us. To put it even more simply: as long as we are not aware of the existence of the natural attitude, or the socially constructed reality frame as a one-dimensional reality that obscures our dimensionality, we simply exist in a consciousness rather than with consciousness.

This is no simple matter, for a consciousness so shared—a consciousness that pervades a world-view to the extent that the individual loses sight of his inherent potential to create personal values based upon subjective awareness and decisions—exhibits an autonomy and willfulness we usually ascribe to an individual personality. That is, such a consciousness moves the group as if it were an organism reacting to an instinctual demand, thereby effectively obliterating all but major attempts to further the nomos in those places where it no longer meets the needs of a time. What I am emphasizing here is that such concepts as "the natural attitude" or the "collective unconscious" are more than philosophical ideas—they are states and conditions that rise above their philosophical status by virtue of their immediacy. The demands of an earlier time that we simply tend to our gardens by following the path of our own individuation as a solution to the collective condition are no longer viable in the face of a world-consciousness accelerated by the autonomy of technology. No more fitting are psychotherapeutic "technologies" that simply attend to maintaining the fabric of the natural attitude, forgetting the philosophical injunction (which is its father and mother, its sperm and womb) that all such considerations must ultimately move in the direction of liberating the soul from its prison, be that prison the body or the body politic.

And here I do not mean to suggest that the natural attitude is

without its worth, that society's attempt to maintain its integrity
is without value, without justification, that it should be dismantled
and all freed from their obligatory enchantment. It *is* necessary.
But is it necessary that psychology become entangled in society's
necessity? In order to operate efficiently society and its members
should be counseled regarding their obligation to one another, to
the issues of community necessary for the machinery of being-in-
the-world. But psychology must instead, or in addition, attend to
its philosophical origins and the directives contained therein: that
the individual be aided in the creation and establishment of his own
nomos—a nomos that allows him to see what it is that he does,
and that he does so by choice rather than by blind obligation. There
a clear demarcation must be drawn between society and the individual's needs which at base have little to do with one another
if the individual's obligations to society have either been satisfac-
torily met or ransomed. At that juncture there must exist a psychology that attends to where the individual has already too much
attended to the "natural" attitude at the expense of his own psyche's
needs: there a psychology must be created to address a nomos of
personal construction backed by both a phenomenological and ex-
istential position that seeks neither to enhance nor diminish anything
within the natural attitude, but rather hopes to add to it addenda
derived from the dialectical quandry posited and resolved precisely
by persons in society. This should have been psychology's goal:
to locate and expiate that aspect of the individual's experience of
himself where necessity has become commandment.

Within the boundaries of the natural attitude, the concept of
"normalcy" is easy to attain (complicated by nothing more than
disagreement), complied with in assurance of inclusion and reward.
Rote agreement empowers the *status quo* position while leading us
toward a stasis that sharply curtails the world-building and compensatory dynamic that makes the human event so unique. The recent didactic romanticism directed towards the non-human world—
represented by monkeys, whales, dolphins, or other variations of
the noble savage—may actually reflect society's fixation with the
stability of physical instinct. We move towards the closed and dictated system of the animal world in the hope that it might resolve
our inherent instability, and in so doing fail to recognize that what
we unwittingly seek to sacrifice is the ongoing creativity of our
condition.

But when one sees and at the same time acknowledges the existence and the needs of the natural attitude, what then? And where is psychology's responsibility to those who have answered that need, and now present a need of their own? Here is where a new psychology is truly imperative, without which the old psychology becomes nothing more than society's socialization program, a religion without vision, basking in the iteration and certitudes of compliance.

If the natural attitude is a given, something we are born into without agreement, and if we are convinced that agreement is not necessary where nomotic acceptance is concerned, one would assume that when society does not work—when an individual does not comply—that either the individual has been dealt a poor socialization program from the onset, or that the imprinted program no longer holds. Then, from a psychotherapeutic viewpoint, a determination must be made concerning not only what society needs, but what the individual needs. Does the individual need restoration, a return to the *status quo* position that he has either inadvertently failed or been failed by, or does the individual need to move on, towards a position that is not normally sanctioned by society's needs? What this implies is that therapy, so practiced, would have to come up against the natural attitude and all of its strictures regarding what therapy as an art should be about. And an art it is, and for that reason, as art, it always should aim at moving itself forward through itself, getting no more stuck in its style than art should or does. But in my estimation, to successfully do so it must first challenge the very thing we have up to this point been implicitly challenging—where exactly does the individual stand in relation to the thing called consciousness, and what exactly is the consciousness he stands in?

From all that has been said so far, it should be apparent that the consciousness of the natural attitude, that into which we are all born and initially agree with, is a form of possession in which we know not what we do but nonetheless do because we believe we must. Jung was quite clear when he stated that this world, the world of the natural attitude, "is a place where mankind is a victim of impulses, instincts, unconsciousness of participation mystique, a dark and unconscious place, a sort of womb . . . . We are just beginning, less than embryos; we are just germs that have to become, like a seed in the womb . . . . When you are just at one with a thing you are completely identical—you cannot comprehend it, you cannot discriminate, you cannot recognize it."[25]

III
An Anthropology of Consciousness

If tendencies toward dissociation were not inherent in the human
psyche, fragmentary psychic systems would never have been split
off: in other words, neither spirits nor gods would have ever come
into existence.

C. G. Jung

If as Jung states it is not we who contain the psyche, but the
psyche that contains us, then we would expect to find the psychological phenomena we usually associate with subjective experience
at the collective level as well. This would mean that neither the collective unconscious nor the archetypes it houses are to be misunder-
stood as transpersonal and extra-mundane realities. It would instead mean that we are intimately and immediately contained within
them, that the better portion of our days are prompted and guided
by both the collective unconscious and the archetypes. In short,
that the location of the unconscious is social reality, and the archetypes the societal roles that live themselves through us.

An example from Greek mythology brings us even closer to the
theme we are discussing; Kerenyi informs us that the goddess
Themis, "she of good counsel," takes her name from *themis*, which
means "a law of nature, the norm of the living together of gods
and beings generally."[26] The goddess simply personifies the norms
of communal living. Jane Harrison is even clearer about the matter
in the following:

> She is the force that brings and binds men together, she is 'herd
> instinct,' the collective conscience, the social sanction . . . . This
> social imperative is among a primitive group diffuse, vague, in-
> choate, yet absolutely binding. Later it crystallizes into fixed con-
> ventions, regular tribal customs; finally in the polis it takes shape
> as Law and Justice. Themis was before the particular shapes of
> gods: she is not religion, but she is the stuff of which religion is
> made. It is the emphasis and representation of herd instinct, of
> the collective conscience, that constitutes religion.[27]

> The Greek word Themis and the English word Doom are philology
> tells us, one and the same . . . . Doom is the thing set, fixed,
> settled; it begins in convention, the stress of public opinion; it
> ends in statutory judgment. Your private doom is your private

opinion, but that is weak and ineffective. It is the collective doom, public opinion, that, for man's common convenience, crystallizes into Law . . . . Out of many dooms, many public opinions, many judgments, arose the figure of the one goddess. Out of many *themistes* arose Themis. These *themistes,* these fixed conventions, stood to the Greek for all he held civilized . . . . These *themistes* are the ordinances of what must be done, what society compels; they are also, because what must be will be, the prophecies of what shall be in the future: they are also the dues, the rites, the prerogatives of a king, whatever custom assigns to him or any official.[28]

The amalgamation of many *themistes* gives birth to a consciousness and a conscience of nuministic proportion because it is representative of collective opinion. Raised to this level and with this end to serve, its autonomous continuance as the carrier of public opinion is then felt, as Kerenyi stated, as a law of nature. From this felt experience it then gains the stature of eternality, transmundanity, and divinity. The personified image does nothing more than alert us to the fact that what we are indeed in the presence of is a force of nature—the nature of society, of humans in commerce with one another, a consciousness created out of this single event, a condition that arises out of communion. Here we see in this brief example how collective opinions coalesce into the personified image of a goddess—an archetype—and the manner by which collectively held views are raised to the level of autonomy and numinosity.

The numinosity surrounding social institutions as felt and personified by the early Greeks and others, is still today expressed in the awe experienced by all when confronted by that which presents itself as supreme and final in its jurisdiction: society. It is in this manner that we become contained in a collective psyche. And because every institution needs actors to carry forth and concretize its principles, the social roles of doctor, nurse, hero, artist, thief, mother, father, child, etc., are created, each with its own nomos. These patterns of action in turn gain the autonomy and eternality of the institutions that define them. These are the archetypes of the collective unconscious, about which Jung writes.

It is indeed hard to see how one can escape the sovereign power of the primordial images. Actually I do not believe it can be escaped. One can only alter one's attitude and thus save oneself from naively falling into an archetype and being forced to act a part at the expense of one's humanity. Possession by an archetype turns a man into a flat collective figure, a mask behind which he can no longer develop as a human being, but becomes increasingly stunted.[29]

Jung is quite clear (if we allow that the primordiality of the images or the archetypes are actually the objectivated meanings we have spoken of earlier), when he states that one cannot escape either these roles or the fact of their existence. As he puts it, one can only alter one's attitude—but such an alternation demands that a recognition of the condition and its depth precede. This implies that one of psychology's major concerns should have been the trumpeting of these socially archetypal facts and the counselling of all who would answer to the gamble of a different path.

I must again emphasize that what is being addressed is immediate: the sovereign, powerful primordial images are those of the institutionalized necessities divinized by their numinosity. It is for this reason that Jung could say that "the archetype fulfills itself not only psychically in the individual, but objectively outside the individual."[30] The archetypes are the institutionalized roles created by the natural attitude, the masks or personaes we are expected to wear, for "What society demands is *imitation* or conscious identification, a treading of accepted, authorized paths."[31]

But because it is within the natural attitude that one becomes identified with the archetype, society's coerciveness is its demand that the individual become identified with a pattern of action, a role, or in other words an archetype. Thus the concept of the norm is developed within the parameters of the natural attitude, in that every society or group is subject to create such a concept, a norm suggesting the existence of an archetype of normalcy whose primary goal is the fulfillment of the collective common need.[32] In turn, the consciousness associated with, and oftentimes a synonym for "normalcy," bears with it the rigidity of attitude and belief that is the *hallmark* of possession by an archetype.[34] The defense system of reality-frames is constructed along the guidelines of such a natural attitude. You cannot have society—no matter how small or how large that society may be—without a concept of what is normal. Wherever and whenever people congregate for whatever reason, they must do so under the umbrella of standardized forms of social participation.[34]

If the natural attitude is achieved through coercive activities, as Freud suggested, we are left with the possibility that coercion is the major if not the sole precipitating fact in pathology. Freud himself suggested this when he wrote that "many people fall ill precisely from an attempt to sublimate their instincts beyond the degree permitted by their organization."[35] That is, the inherent organization of the instincts demands a certain quantum of expression. Their repression, in all or in part, distorts or discredits the integrity of their organization. It is this, Freud implies, that causes one to fall psychologically ill. It might therefore be this coercive (but albeit, necessary) societal demand that creates the medium necessary for deviant and pathological behavior to express itself. However, let us not jump to entertaining utopian programs of social reform that would forever eliminate the pressures society brings to bear on some individuals.

> . . . in any society, it would be inevitable that a percentage (itself variable) of individuals find themselves placed 'off system,' so to speak, or between two or more irreducible systems. The group seeks and even requires of those individuals that they figuratively represent certain forms of compromise which are not realisable on the collective plane; that they simulate imaginary transitions, embody incompatible syntheses. So, in all their apparently aberrant modes of behavior, individuals who are 'ill' are just transcribing a state of the group, and making one or another of its constants manifest.[36]

Therefore, wherever society is to be found we can expect to find pathology as well, for it is an integral part of society's process. Without the socially determined demarcation of this process the whole of society falls anyway.[37] We could therefore say that pathologies are social states that reflect society's inability to legitimize certain types of behavior through the election of vocation.[38]

In other words, pathologies, or the states we define as such, are a necessary element in the creation and maintenance of social equilibrium achieved within the parameters of the natural attitude. Those statistical findings that indicate correspondence between mental illnesses and social classes therefore suggest that the results of repressive activities are peculiar to the dynamics of each class.[39] With these strong indications that a great number of pathologies fall within the specific boundaries of social class, we can assume that class structure either nominates or determines the quality of certain psychological experiences which are to be defined as pathological. That is, "psychological" illnesses reflect deviance from the group's concept of normality for the reasons Lévi-Strauss stated: they transcribe a component of the group. Because such concepts are culture—and class—specific and therefore determined by social agreement (some acts deemed deviant or pathological in one group being but the norm for another),[40] they are also models by which individuals present their plight to others—that is, they are again archetypal in that they are models of behavior that (in this instance) differentiate socially prescribed patterns of protest.

Insofar as "every archetype is capable of infinite development and differentiation . . . [and] therefore [it is] possible for it to be more developed or less,"[41] the archetype itself cannot be thought of as a static and fixed modality. If pathologies are archetypal in structure, for the reasons explained above, then they may very well be the attempts of those archetypes that define the parameters of the natural attitude, and therefore of the norm, to individuate. Those who become identified with the individuating intent of the archetype are "individuals who, for social, historical or physiological reasons (it does not matter which), are sensitive to the contradictions and gaps in social structure; and our society hands over to those individuals the task of realising a statistical equivalent (by constituting that complement, 'abnormality,' which alone can supply a definition of 'the normal'."[42] If the collective psyche is truly as autonomous as theory and observation appear to indicate, it is more than feasible that it would attempt to maintain its integral need to *be*—and it would do so through individuals positioned in such a manner as to invite such compensatory possession. While the autonomy of the archetypes is a recognized fact in Jungian logos, that they themselves individuate (aside from fulfilling Jung's intimation regarding that they are capable of infinite development) has never been considered. Yet, individuation, as a rule, is an unconscious process, rarely attaining consciousness without willed intervention.[43] Thus there is every reason to suspect that individuation would be, by definition, camouflaged; i.e., intrinsically self-obscuring and phenomenologically self-nullifying. Jung himself stated that whenever the collective dominants or archetypes failed a culture, images of individuation set in.[44] He added, however, that this failure inevitably leads to a possession by the archetypes in which the "possessed identify themselves with the archetypal contents of their unconscious . . . [and] exemplify these concretely in their own lives, thus becoming prophets and reformers."[45] I would here amend Jung's statement (that such individuals become possessed by the archetypal contents of *their* own unconscious) by referring the reader back to the idea that the dominants of the unconscious are actually internalized "roles" of society. With this amendment in mind, we see that the possession he speaks of complements Lévi-Strauss's observation that such individuals are simply "sensitive to the contradictions and gaps in the social structure," serving as conduits for society's individuation.

I have on several occasions employed the term "possession" to define a state illustrative of the condition in which an individual, or a group, acts in accord with principles arising solely out of societal demands or needs, rather than decisions based upon subjective analysis and self-determination. To most, the term smacks of primitivism, of situations removed from our modern reality. But in point of fact, possession states are the very essence of what psychology presently concerns itself with. Even the most cursory survey of the history of psychological theories will substantiate this. However, whereas most historians point to the parallelisms readily inferred between modern classifications and their ancient counterparts, emphasizing the similarity in symptomatology, only Jung (in my estimation) has presented a clear picture of the modern presence of this condition:

> Psychoneuroses and psychoses have from time immemorial been regarded as states of *possession* . . .
>
> I would use it [the term possession] in a much wider sense as designating a frequently occurring psychic phenomenon: any autonomous complex not subject to the conscious will exerts a possessive effect on consciousness proportional to its strength and limits the latter's freedom.[46]

Thus, possession states need not be overt caricatures of personality-loss or disorientation—which they sometimes are as in schizophrenia and multiple-personality disorders—but states as simple as those outlined by Freud in his *The Psychopathology of Everyday Life*, in which the forgetting of names, slips of the tongue and other such "mistakes" were reviewed against the backdrop of unconscious autonomy. Insofar as our concern is primarily with possession as a collective phenomenon, it would profit us to review the structure and dynamics of possession cults.

IV
On the Consciousness of Initiation

The training analysis . . . is not complete until the candidate produces memories, thoughts, and feelings in a form that confirms
the doctrines of the institute.
                                        Jerome D. Frank

The founding members of such cults always undergo an ordeal
of breakdown, dissolution, and return or recuperation. In cultures
where such cults are a permanent and institutional feature, the prere-
quisites for their leadership acquire traditional features. For example, in those cultures where shamanism plays a prominent role, a
specific set of crisis-circumstances must be present in order to satisfy
nomination to such a leadership position.[47] Whether such crisis-
circumstances are socially delineated or not, the individual in either
primitive or modern settings always goes through an experience
others in his group would describe as either unusual and/or difficult. As indicated, where such a cult has been pre-established, the
crisis follows specific guidelines, the fulfillment of which guarantees
membership. In other words, the illness or crisis replicates the experience of earlier initiates, if not the founder himself and what we
are witness to is a culturally determined and induced "illness." The
breakdown experience having been successfully maneuvered, the
cult then promises to provide a new nomos whereby the initiate
might resuscitate or finally gain access to the power and position
originally denied him. Without exception, the benefits afforded the
individual arise from knowledge of a very particular and privileged
form—a knowledge equated with power of a mystical, magical or
metaphysical nature.[48]
    Simply put, the individual must first experience a breakdown
of his reality-frame which results in, as I have noted earlier, an
altered state of consciousness that is religious in tone.[49] The cult,
as the socially sanctioned container for such events, then appro-
priates the individual's experience as justification for its existence
as an institution bearing secret wisdom. In time, "the more strongly-
based and entrenched religious authority becomes, the more hostile
it is towards haphazard inspiration,"[50] thereby strengthening the
internal structure and social power of the organization. If successful,
the cult will become recognized by society as a legitimate institu-

tion.[51]

Without exception, possession cults occupy the lower social strata of a group or culture and are populated by individuals who (for a variety of reasons) have not been allowed the channels of self-government or power the *status quo* members of their culture enjoy.[52] The majority of their members in primitive cultures are women; in civilized cultures that are more diverse in population those factors that initially contribute to prejudicial classifications play the more prominent role—in Western culture, so-called minority groups.

Erika Bourguignon informs us that possession falls into two categories: trance possession and non-trance possession. In trance possession the individual allows a total displacement of his personality in favor of a takeover by a spirit or a deity. Because "types of societies which exert strong pressures for compliance are also those where we expect to find possession trance," in those societies where "one succeeds by being obedient, responsible, and nurturant, in short by being compliant . . . the individual enhances his power and his status by total abdication and self-effacement before the spirits. . . . He can achieve dominance and assertion only indirectly, through the unconscious pretense of obedience and submission."[53]

The Tonga women of the Zambesi valley are a case in point. The appearance of European industry in the vicinity drew their husbands away from their village to a nearby town where they met native women who had been influenced by the soaps and perfumes of Western culture, abandoning the traditional oil and ochre of the Valley women. The village women, faced with the threat of losing their husbands, became possessed by spirits that demanded that the husbands supply their wives with the accoutrements that the town-women enjoyed.[54] Here we are clearly presented with the rationale behind both non-trance and trance possession: the acquisition of attention through the power inherent in demands made by spiritual and transpersonal agencies on behalf of those possessed. It is in such a manner that oppressed groups, or groups denied access to socially prescribed types of relationships, achieve power.[55]

Non-trance possession cults are no different in their attempts to acquire power; they too are composed of individuals who are at the lower end of the social structure. However, non-trance possession cults arise only in cultures "which exert strong pressure toward assertion."[56] This type of individual does not acquire power by either impersonation of spirits, or an abdication of his personality, but rather through a relationship with the spirit that is "not dependent upon the group . . . [and is] most likely obtained . . . on his own, in his own dealing with the spirit. Nontrance possession represents an alteration of the individual's capacities, not an alteration of his consciousness. In societies which socialize for assertion, such an alteration of capacities results from the interaction of independent, self-reliant human beings with spirits or powers of limited capacities."[57]

In addition, all such cults—known as cults of affliction because the initiates must initially present themselves as afflicted—become healing cults which on the one hand attract initiates with disorders corresponding to those of the original founder, and on the other create healers out of those "cured" by the disorders which were a prerequisite for their membership.

Inasmuch as there have always been and will always be individuals who either do not, or feel they do not, have access to knowledge and power, one can assume that there will always be cults whose function is to promote self-esteem. But not every cult becomes a major social institution such as Christianity. It appears that the institutionalization of a cult demands that the culture in which it is founded must itself first go through a crisis, a breakdown of its reality-frame. As in a personal breakdown, an upsurge of and recourse to mystical experiences becomes manifest via a proliferation of cult activity. We can assume that any metaphysical program that answers or compensates the culture in crisis may be turned to as a vehicle of rejuvenation and stabilization. Such a situation existed between 2 B.C. and 2 A.D., and gave rise to Christianity as the moral and ethical program of salvation.

V
"As a Thief in the Night."

. . . mental-health problems are not medical but human—that is,
economic, moral, social, and political problems. In other words,
mental illnesses are metaphorical diseases.
Thomas Szasz

One of the major events that gave birth to the modern idea of consciousness and the therapy that promulgates it, aside from other equally important historical antecedents that have been well documented, was the Industrial Revolution, the major feature of which was the shifting of attention away from the technique of production to the industrial organization of that production. Village home-industries that had existed since the Middle Ages were relocated in factories,[58] thereby effectively destroying cottage industries as well as the dynamics of the nuclear family. Breakthrough may have provoked inventions that called for and supported this organizational shift, but new methods and procedures in agricultural production had been set in motion two centuries earlier and these radically transformed patterns of individual land ownership in England—the parent of the Revolution. The first step in this transformation occurred during the sixteenth century "enclosure movement," which sought "to make the land carry more sheep for the wool trade."[59] The second, initiated at the end of the eighteenth century, called for the enclosure of common land for the production of greater crops. This last act forced the home worker, who depended upon the common lands for the grazing of his small flock and as the source of wood for fuel, to move from the village into industrial towns where he then became cheap labor. The creation of a labor force necessitated the disintegration of the family as an autonomous and independent unit and the breakdown of moral codes that had existed continuously for centuries. This breakdown occurred with the introduction, at a collective level, of a public life whose codes differed from that of private life. Prior to this time personal morality and public behavior were inseparable. In addition, the extraction of males from the family unit to satisfy the industrial needs of this new public arena created a new hierarchy in which the family became dependent upon the successful public life of fathers and sons.

Mothers and sisters, on the other hand, while experiencing what to them was total and eternal exclusion from the inherent power afforded men's entry into this newly created arena, were also relegated to an even more servile and dependent position. Not only did they become totally responsible for the maintenance of the home, but also for the child-rearing responsibilities that had once been shared with the men in the family. This latter status would in time lead to psychoanalytical statements such as, "clinically it . . . [follows] that all mental conflicts concerned the relation of the child to its mother."[60] What must be stressed is the lack of autonomy and power offered women and the degree to which this outcome aided considerably the very creation of the psychoanalytical movement. The socioeconomic plight of women and its inevitable complaints would be described by Freud and his followers within the context of penis-envy:

> From the analysis of many neurotic women we have learnt that women go through an early phase in which they envy their brothers the token of maleness and feel themselves handicapped and ill-treated on account of the lack of it (really, on account of its diminutive form). In our view this 'penis-envy' forms part of the castration complex. If 'masculine' is to include the connotation of 'wishing to be masculine,' the term 'masculine protest' fits this attitude; this term was coined by Alfred Adler for the purpose of proclaiming this factor as the foundation of all neurosis in general. During this early phase little girls often make no secret of their envy of the favoured brother, and the animosity it gives to against him; they even try to urinate standing upright like the brother, thus asserting the equality with him they claim.[61]

As can be surmised, the envy that sisters felt towards their brothers had essentially to do with the access males had to avenues of self-reliance and power women were not allowed. Daughters were raised with the full knowledge that what lay ahead for them was simply a transfer from their fathers' family into that of their husbands'. Sons on the other hand were raised with the assumed certainty of transfer from the confines of family into a public life where they could be assured a modicum of freedom and self-determination through competition. In short, following the distinctions between trance and non-trance personalities, women were raised for compliance, men for self-assertion; women were raised in a manner that (in primitive cultures) gives rise to trance possession. While it is more than likely true that women in both primitive and European cultures have always been placed in compliant positions, the original amalgamation of both private and public sectors within the confines of a group, village, or township allowed them, in one manner or another, directly to impact male society with their protests. With the total isolation of the males by their inclusion in a public sector, such impact, if possible at all, was negligible. And yet we can safely assume that the need to protest, as a form of autonomous psychological venting, occurred nonetheless. That Freud's first clients were women displaying the symptoms of hysteria has been stressed by James Hillman as the birth of psychoanalysis.[62] Freud himself made the comparison between hysteria and possession in the following:

> Let no one object that the theory of dissociation of consciousness as a solution of the enigma of hysteria is too-far-fetched to suggest itself to the untrained and unprejudiced observer. In fact the Middle Ages had chosen this very solution, in declaring possession by a demon to be the cause of hysterical manifestations; all that would have been required was to replace the religious terminology of those dark and superstitious times by the scientific one of to-day.[63]

Clearly, Freud understood hysteria as not only a state of possession coinciding with our definition of trance possession, but also as a form of protest in that it had a motive which "is, of course, invariably the gaining of some advantage . . . . In the first place, falling ill involves a saving of psychical effort; it emerges as being economically the most convenient solution when there is a mental conflict . . . . But beyond this external factors (such as . . . the situation of a woman subjugated by her husband) may contribute motives for falling ill."[64]

We could therefore say that Freud's formulation of his psychoanalytic process grew out of a response to the crisis created by the Industrial Revolution in which the position of and the relationship between men and women was radically altered. It was in essence a therapy that aimed at adapting sons to the new world of their fathers in preparation for their future role as fathers.[65] For women, psychoanalysis set out to explain, via pseudo-anthropological data and to the total exclusion of socio-economic facts, that their condition was dependent and submissive by virtue of their failed sexuality.[66] In addition, the autonomy men entertained was achieved by the rationalization and control of affect necessary to maintain public personae, leading to the situation in which "individual autonomy and inclusion presupposed a fundamental split between public and private realms of feeling."[67] It was in such a manner that the Western psyche gave birth to a split psyche in which ethical values between public and private life inevitably clash—an issue Jung would repeatedly address in his psychology.[68] As we have seen, the Industrial Revolution aided in the rupturing of the reality-frame of the West. The event we have outlined eventually led to the demarcation of compliant and non-compliant personalities within practically every family in the Western world—and a psychology that on the one hand supported the split while on the other (through "treatment") sought to maintain it.[69]

I have in these pages outlined the societal fabric out of which the original psychoanalytic patient was woven, suggesting that contrary to academic and popular beliefs little has changed between primitive and modern forms of recruitment for psychological treatment: therapy, primitive or modern, essentially caters to protest responses, and in this regard is an inestimably valuable course to follow for the maintenance of the social nomos. But my question here is: What of the individual when he stands aside from his social status? And the equally important: Who am I, rather than simply What am I?

VI
The Cult of Consciousness

. . . we lack all knowledge of the unconscious psyche and pursue the cult of consciousness to the exclusion of all else. Our true religion is a monotheism of consciousness.
C. G. Jung

The materials presented in the above sections addressed the phenomena that at first sight appeared to exist only within the realms of anthropological interests, having little to do with the vissicitudes of modern life in the Western world. We addressed the idea that modern concepts of psychopathology and primitive theories of possession appeared to correspond to one another. Our outline of trance and non-trance possession phenomena, along with the social dynamics that give rise to such states, restricted itself to so-called primitive cultures. As our last section suggested, the appearance of both modern and primitive healing cults is a compensatory response to the crisis that the natural attitude is threatened by from time to time. Often, such therapies support and justify the equilibrium the collective social psyche seeks to maintain via the creation and maintenance of a norm. To all appearances, the norm is established and determined by a collective adjustment to situations that have arisen because of social crisis. That is, the inequities created, for example, by the social demands placed upon the family at the time of the Industrial Revolution, were "explained" by psychoanalytic theory. Explanations are often justifications, and any therapy that bases its efficacy solely on explanation will serve simply to maintain the newly acquired condition of the *status quo*. When we attended to the description of the types of societies that give birth to trance and non-trance phenomena, we saw that this classificatory system could easily explain the politics of the family that arose around the turn of the century. Psychoanalysis was created in an attempt to explain the new condition, and then set out to maintain the very condition that was symptomatic of a lesion in society.

Insofar as correlations are to be founded between specific types of disorders and class position, we can also assume that family systems follow class expectations. In any given culture, therefore, one will find therapies that will define types of distress as forms of mental illness because they fail to comply with the types of social behavior appropriate to that society or class system.[70] By the same token, however, individuals attempting to protest by adopting the social postures (pathologies) deemed appropriate to their group will seek to display symptomatology that has been guaranteed to receive special and specific types of attention. This is more than likely the reason why, according to sociological surveys, schizophrenia has a statistically higher incidence in the lower classes, and affective disorders the higher. Individuals in the lower classes tend to be placed or forced into positions of compliance because of either socioeconomic, racial, or religious reasons: Thus, we would expect to find psychological phenomena in accord with trance possession as opposed to the affective disorders of the upper classes, who, as a rule, train for self-reliance and assertiveness—and perhaps attain their social position because of propensities towards this form of extraverted activity. From this we can also assume that each class or group has its own definition of normality or consciousness, and that these latter concepts are moderated and adjusted by therapeutic techniques that ultimately seek to adjust the individual to his cultural milieu.[71]

What we must attend to now is the fact that, at the very least, there are three major types of societal responses to possession phenomena I have linked to modern definitions of pathology. Bourguignon is again helpful in delineating these responses by defining the societies in which they are found:

(1) Societies where the behavior is desired and often intentionally induced, (2) societies where the behavior is feared and vigorous efforts are made to drive out the spirit supposed to be in a residence (often with physical violence) and, (3) perhaps most interesting, societies where the initial spontaneous behavior is considered deviant and perhaps sick, and where a cure involves bring-

ing about possession trance in a controlled setting. Therapy, in this last category, does not consist in stopping the possession-trance behavior but, as it were, in domesticating it, in developing a new personality and a new status in society. Here, the possession-trance illness and cure in fact constitute a form of religious initiation. The ability to work through a personal psychological crisis in a culturally acceptable way makes the experience one of personality growth and reorganization.

A phenomenon which would have been disruptive to both the sufferer and the society is used as a social asset rather than as a liability. The rituals of therapy and the acquisition of new ritual status by the new cult member or shaman thus are methods of social adaption.[72]

Jung's insistence that to be without a neurosis, or a possession, would be to be without a point in life, and his position that a neurosis contains a bit of undeveloped personality,[73] corresponds to the last society Bourguignon defined. It is here where the entire issue of possession and normality hinges, and where a necessary discrimination must be made—for possession by the archetype of "normalcy" and possession by or inclusion of the "new personality" refer us to two entirely different sets or conditions. One therapeutic move returns the individual to the collective condition of the natural attitude in which the sacrifice of a certain portion of his personality is demanded, whereas in the other such sacrifice is refused in favor of becoming what one is *as one is*.[74] It is this latter course that demands the neurosis be borne along so that the undeveloped portion of personality may be realized. This undeveloped portion is contained in the complex which Jung has described as a "little personality," that is ostensibly autonomous, with a will and life of its own—as a type of possession.[75] That he also feels "this personification of complexes is not in itself necessarily a pathological condition,"[76] punctuates Jung's allegiance with Bourguignon's third societal attitude towards possession. It should also be apparent that trance possession, or what Jung refers to as a cured state achieved through a sacrifice of some portion of personality, answers the goals of the second society she describes. That the individual is returned to the natural attitude and the fullfilment of socially determined archetypal roles suggests trance possession by virtue of the fact that something of the individual must be given up or displaced. The other course Jung outlines suggests a non-trance personality situation, which answers the description of a potentially individuating personality:

Because individuation begins with the rigid persona and proceeds to release the repressed (collective) inner core of the self, it progressively divests the person of his participation in publicly determined roles and behavior . . . . The end point of individuation is a pure and intensely privatized self, liberated from all obligation imposed from without by the social order . . . . Of course the individual self retains its persona, but the persona is secondary when compared with the self.[77]

In this therapeutic instance the alternation of attitude necessary to protect one from identification with an archetype not only aids one in the differentiation from that archetype, but in consciously assimilating the fact of the archetype's existence—becoming aware of where in our personalities we have become self-identified with it and therefore lost the opportunity of experiencing the potentials inherent in the condition we call our humanity.

If we may define Freud's psychology, along with all those psychologies that in any manner find their philosophical basis in psychoanalytic theory, as a "normalizing" psychology that returns the individual to the natural attitude, then we may also refer to Jung's psychology, along with any of its developments or revisions, as a psychology that in the final analysis moves towards "individuation." A normalizing psychology, therefore, adjusts those individuals who have slipped outside of the norm and, in having done so, experience discomfort because of their exclusion from the group. An individuating psychology attends to those who do not fully meet the demands of the norm, and either cannot or wish not to be returned or included in the group—who will not sacrifice what they experience as unique. The normalizing therapies would therefore cater to and base their central principles on the trance possession type of personality. Thus, all manner of addictions, compulsive, obsessive, and anxiety types of neurosis would not only be best served by such therapies, but would also define the therapeutic objectives of such therapies—return and restoration. The individuating therapies would appear to work most efficiently with individuals displaying personality styles reminiscent of personality disorders, if not the disorders themselves. I do not mean to suggest that those who seek either of these therapies in an attempt to resolve their difficulties display the pathologies outlined, but rather that the therapies as we here define them, because of their philosophical positions and perspectives, best serve the disorders mentioned. That individuals with specific types of disorders would also be drawn to psychologies that in essence recognize, give credence, and aid to their complaints, is assumed. Nonetheless, we cannot lose sight of the fact that both the normalizing and individuating therapies attend to two types of possession—one trance and the other non-trance. That is, they are therapies whose calling and intent is the administering to those who have in their estimation or in the estimation of others, failed some major facet of the norm.

The modern split that was created in society because of the events that took place at the beginning of the twentieth century, was accompanied by a compensating metaphysic—psychology. I call it a metaphysic because it does not directly address the issues of a consciousness *of* reality, but instead offers a definition of a compensated reality *called* consciousness. It informs us how we should respond to being in society, rather than, or in addition to, the response to Being in itself. It suggests that society must be adhered to in every circumstance regardless of the inequities sometimes inherent in such accommodation. In short, it asks us to think of psyche—psychology—as something divorced from the immediacy of the quest of being in favor of an adjustment to societal demands alone. But we can expect nothing better from psychologies that suggest the dynamics of the psyche can or should be understood as universal under all conditions, for what they ostensibly aim at are programs of universal socialization along the guidelines of norms that are by their very nature only applicable to the culture in which they have been produced. While we may here agree that at base the human psyche is universal in composition, we must also allow that it is also universally malleable and molded by the specific needs of the milieu within which it has been contained and socialized. That on the whole psychology calls for an homogenized view of the psyche simply points to another attempt to find closure in our condition, to discover in our condition—our simple being—meaning. But we cannot expect to find meaning in structures and strictures that define our being; that prompt nothing but socially determined patterns of action. A philosophical position is needed that not only recognizes and serves both the realities of the natural attitude and the individuating perspective, but that is also capable of working beyond the parameters of trance and non-trance possession that these positions respectively exemplify. *That* psychology would have to be capable of judiciously determining which side of the split the individual operates from, as well as producing a therapy that moves beyond the archetypally inherent divisiveness that every traditional theory of consciousness bears.

The psychologies that presently exist tend to mythologize reality, divinizing it so that it may give us meaning. In the normalizing therapies we are returned to the collective myths. In the individuating therapies we are informed that the peculiarities of our possession are positive because we do not return to the collective myth but instead enter and fully participate in specialized and often exclusive myths. In both instances we are presented with definitions of consciousness arising out of a perception of reality that does not attend to or comply with either the expected or socially determined—in other words, the norm. To the extent that we comply solely with these psychological definitions, we have lost contact with a philosophical enquiry into being that asks a simpler and more difficult question: what is Being from an existent's experience of his experience—and in turn, what is consciousness?

NOTES

[1] ". . . consciousness is characterized by the mobilization of a structured frame of reference in the background of attention which supports, interprets, and gives meaning to all experiences. This frame of reference . . . [is] called the usual generalized reality orientation." Ronald E. Shor, "Hypnosis and the Concept of the Generalized Reality-Orientation," in Charles T. Tart, ed., *Altered States of Consciousness*, Charles T. Tart, ed., New York: John Wiley & Sons, Inc., 1969, p. 236.
This frame of reference, or reality frame as I would prefer to call it, to a considerable degree answers Edmund Husserl's description of the "natural attitude," where "to live is always to live-in-the-certainty-of-the-world." Edmund Husserl, *The Crisis of European Sciences and Transcendental Phenomenology*, Evanston: Northwestern University Press, 1970, p. 142.

[2] *ibid.*, p. 246.

[3] Arthur J. Deikman, "Deautomatization and the Mystic Experience," *ibid.*, p. 30.

[4] Michel Foucault, *Madness & Civilization*, New York: Vintage Books, 1973, p. 33.

[5] "Our contention is that mind can never find expression, and could never have come into existence at all, except in terms of a social environment:

that an organized set or pattern of social relations and interactions (especially those of communication by means of gestures functioning as significant symbols and thus creating a universe of discourse) is necessarily presupposed by it and involved in its nature." George Herbert Mead, *Self and Society*, Charles W. Morris, ed., Chicago/London: The University of Chicago Press, 1962, p. 223.

[6]Sigmund Freud, *The Future of an Illusion*, W. D. Robson-Scott, trans., James Strachey ed., New York: Anchor Books, 1964, p. 3.

[7]*ibid.*, pp. 2–3.

[8]*ibid.*, p. 5.

[9]*ibid.*, p. 20.

[10]*ibid.*, p. 13.

[11]*ibid.*,

[12]*ibid.*, p. 14.

[13]Peter Berger, *The Sacred Canopy: Elements of a Sociological Theory of Religion*, New York: Anchor Books, 1969, p. 4. This dialectic is arrived at via three stages or steps that occur simultaneously, the internalization Freud spoke of being the "final" step. The first, externalization, is "the ongoing outpouring of human being into the world, both in the physical and mental activity of men." The second, objectivation, "is the attainment by the products of this activity (again both physical and mental) of a reality that confronts its original producers as a facticity external to and other than themselves." And finally, internalization which is "the reappropriation by men of this same reality, transforming it once again from structures of the objective world into structures of the subjective consciousness . . . . It is through externalization that society is a human product. It is through objectivation that society becomes a reality *sui generis*. It is through internalization that man is a product of society." *ibid.*

[14]Maurice Natanson, *Edmund Husserl: Philosopher of Infinite Tasks*, Evanston: Northwestern University Press, 1973, p. 22.

[15]"Internalization is rather the reabsorption into consciousness of the objectivated world in such a way that the structures of this world come to determine the subjective structures of consciousness itself. That is, society now functions as the formative agency for individual consciousness." Berger, *op. cit.*, pp. 14–15.

[16]Thomas Szasz, "Models of Madness," in *The Therapeutic State*, Buffalo, New York: Prometheus Books, 1984, pp. 22-27.

[17]Berger, 1969, p. 12.

[18]*ibid.*, 29ff.

[19]*ibid.*, p. 14. The most recent example of all this is to be found in our assumptions regarding the nature of the "masculine" and the "feminine," and what they purportedly tell us about being male and female. Every society defines the difference between the sexes through role assignments, and then in time employs these assignments as *definitions* of what an appropriate male or female is. We achieve this not only through our religious, political, and philosophical positions but perpetuate it through our storytelling. Fairy tales and folktales used to be the vehicles by which we socialized both men and women. Thus, the tale of "Beauty and the Beast," not only informs us that the female should patiently abide with what is beastial in her mate—love in time curing all things—but that men can reside in their beastiality knowing that they will be cured by the ministrations and patience of a loving woman. The old social message in this tale—supported by those religious institutions that speak of marriage as an eternal condition—remains with us in the psychology and pathology of both battered women and men. In the midst of tales that we are informed signify liberation, we find the hidden message of socialization. One could say that the greater portion of television, cinematic and dramatic entertainment, is but an aesthetic presentation of objectivated social prescriptions that have replaced the old fairy/folktale program. Several years ago a television program was created in which the hero was turned by his anger into an enormous, senseless, and violent green giant. The message was quite simple: anger turns us into senseless beasts, and the only time we should give expression to anger is when our lives or the lives of others are endangered. Even then, we are beasts unless we can turn the other cheek. It is through these imaginal constructions that the messages of socialization maintain the internalization of society's dictates.

[20]*ibid.*, p. 15.

[21]"At this point, always assuming a degree of successful socialization, introspection becomes a viable method for the discovery of institutional meanings." Berger, 1969, p. 18.

[22]Berger, 1967, p. 133.

[23]C. G. Jung, "Two Posthumous Papers," *Spring*, 1970, p. 175.

[24]I can think of no culture that does not have a dream-theory, which states itself pro or con the value of dreams in everyday reality, i.e., from cultures that discover value and direction in the dream (Western cultures in particular), to cultures that devalue the dream and qualify liberation through the absence of dreams (Tibetan and other Oriental cultures). What we are faced with in the West is the possibility that the internalization of society's proscriptions may operate through the agency of the dream. In other words, the dream, along with the interpretive systems that arise in an attempt to give or include it in a nomos, may be the vehicle by which the natural attitude maintains itself. This is more than likely the reason why "the dreams of a group of dreamers of the same culture and the same society will likely show some clear regularities in manifest content." (David Schneider & Lauriston Sharp, "The Dream Life of a Primitive People: The Dreams of the vir voron of Australia," in *Anthropological Studies #1*, Ward Goodenough, ed., American Anthropological Association, Ann Arbor, Michigan: University Microfilms, 1969, p. 14. Schneider and Sharp noted that in those dreams presenting images of successful sexual intercourse, the male dreamer's sex partner was of the "appropriate" social category. In those instances where she was not, interruptions of the sexual act occurred, and "the magnitude of the interruption correlates with the strength of the prohibition on sexual relations." *ibid.*, p. 51.

[25]C. G. Jung, "Psychological Commentary on Kundalini Yoga," *Spring*, 1975, pp. 9, 16, 19.

[26]Carl Kerenyi, *The Gods of the Greeks*, London: Thames and Hudson, 1974, p. 102.

[27]Jane Harrison, *Themis*, London: Merlin Press, 1977, p. 485.

[28]*ibid.*, p. 483.

[29]C. G. Jung, *CW*, vol. 7, Princeton: Princeton University Press, 1977, para. 389–90.

[30]C. G. Jung, *CW*, vol. 11, Princeton: Princeton University Press, 1969, para. 648.

[31]C. G. Jung, *Spring*, 1970, p. 174.

[32]James Hillman has alerted us to one aspect of this archetype in his comments regarding Athene Mater as the normalizing principle: "When the soul is examined from an institutional standpoint or approached with conventional thinking and feeling, the perspective operating is that of Athene." James Hillman, "On the Necessity of Abnormal Psychology: Ananke and

Athene," in *Facing the Gods*, James Hillman, ed., Irving, Texas: Spring Publications, Inc., 1980, p. 28.

[33]"The characteristic feature of a pathological reaction is, above all, *identification* with the archetype. This produces a sort of inflation and possession . . . " C. G. Jung, *CW*, vol. 9i, New York: Pantheon Books, 1959, para. 621.

[34]" . . . strictly speaking, the person whom we call sane is the one who is capable of alienating himself, since he consents to an existence in a world definable only by the self-other relationship." Claude Lévi-Strauss, *Introduction to the Work of Marcel Mauss*, London: Routledge & Kegan Paul, 1987, p. 18. Lévi-Strauss here refers to the conclusions of J. Lacan in his "Aggressivity in psychoanalysis."

[35]Sigmund Freud, 1912, p. 119.

[36]Lévi-Strauss, *op. cit.*, p. 18.

[37]"Their [the ill] peripheral position relative to a local system does not mean that they are not integral parts of the total system; they are, and just as much as the local system is. To be more precise, if they were not docile witnesses of this sort, the total system would be in danger of disintegrating into its local systems. It can therefore be said that for every society the relation between normal and special modes of behaviour is one of complementarity." *ibid.*, pp. 18–19.

[38]"That is obvious in the case of shamanism and spirit-possession; but it would be no less true of modes of behaviour which our own society refuses to group and legitimitize as *vocations*." *ibid.*, p. 19.

[39]cf. August B. Hollingshead and Fredrick C. Redlich, *Social Class & Mental Illness*, New York: John Wiley & Sons, Inc., 1958; H. Warren Dunham, *Sociological Theory & Mental Disorder*, Detroit, Michigan: Wayne State University Press, 1959; Don C. Gibbons & Joseph F. Jones, *The Study of Deviance*, Englewood Clifs, New Jersey: Prentice-Hall, Inc., 1975; Robert B. Edgerton, *Deviance: A Cross-Cultural Perspective*, Menlo Park, California, Cummings Publishing Co., 1976; Anthony F. C. Wallace, "Mental Illness, Biology and Culture," in *Psychological Anthropology*, Francis L. K. Hsu, ed., Cambridge, Mass.: Schenkman Publishing Co., Inc., 1972, pp. 363–402. This is in accord with at least one anthropologist's observation that "possession beliefs and rituals [pathologies] . . . reflect and express both social structure and the personalities of the participants." Erika Bourguignon, *Possession*, San Francisco: Chandler & Sharo Publishers, Inc., 1976, p. 49.

[40]For example, cf. Gananath Obeyesekere, "Depression, Buddhism, and the Work of Culture in Sri Lanka," in *Culture and Depression: Studies in the Anthropology and Cross-Cultural Psychiatry of Affect and Disorder,"* Arthur Kleinman and Byron Good, editors, Berkeley: University of California Press, 1985, pp. 134–152, where the author stresses that modern Western psychiatric definitions of a depressed person describe what in Sri Lanka would be identified as the qualities of a good Buddhist.

[41]C. G. Jung, *CW,* vol. 12, London: Routledge & Kegan Paul, 1953, para. 12.

[42]Lévi-Strauss, *op. cit.,* p. 19.

[43]C. G. Jung, *CW,* vol. 11, *op. cit.,* para. 755–6.

[44]In discussing the emergence of Gnosticism, Jung states that it "was founded on the perception of symbols thrown up by the process of individuation which always sets in when the collective dominants of human life fall into decay." C. G. Jung, *CW,* vol. 12, *op. cit.,* para. 41. We can assume that such is the case during any period in history experiencing a breakdown.

[45]*ibid.* Whereas Jung is here discussing the emergence of Gnosticism as a response to ideas in Classical religions that had become obsolete, we must keep in mind that many so-called prophets and reformers in both the past and the present, insofar as they do not fully answer the needs of a society's dilemma during a time of crisis or transition, inevitably fall into the category of the pathological. Our mental institutions are filled with such prophets, and our daily newspapers are filled with mention of those who, because of the tenacity of their egos, have yet to fall. Thus, that which is determined to be pathological in a culture may also be viewed as attempts on the part of society, or the natural attitude, to correct itself in the face of outmoded social ways of being.

[46]C. G. Jung, *CW,* vol. 11, *op. cit.,* para. 242, ftnote #15; also see, C. G. Jung, *CW,* vol. 16, New York: Pantheon Books, 1954, par. 196.

[47]" . . . all the ecstatic experiences that determine the future shaman's vocation involve the traditional schema of an initiation ceremony: suffering, death, resurrection. Viewed from this angle, any 'sickness vocation' fills the role of an initiation: for the sufferings that it brings on correspond to initiatory tortures, the psychic isolation of the 'elected' is the counterpart to the isolation and ritual solitude of initiation ceremonies, and the imminence of death felt by the sick man (pain, unconsciousness, etc.) recalls the symbolic death represented in almost all initiation ceremonies." Mircea Eliade, *Shamanism: Archaic Techniques of Ecstasy,* Princeton: Princeton University Press, 1964, p. 33.

[48]cf. Marcel Mauss, *A General Theory of Magic*, New York: W. W. Norton & Co., 1975, p. 29.

[49]cf. Arthur J. Deikman, *op. cit.*, pp. 23–43.

[50]I. M. Lewis, *Ecstatic Religion: An Anthropological Study of Spirit Possession and Shamanism*, Maryland: Penguin Books, 1971, p. 34.

[51]An example close at hand is the Christian Church's beginnings as a small cult of twelve members that eventually flowered into an institution capable of influencing every facet of life in millions of members throughout the world.

[52]"What we find over and over again in a wide range of different cultures and places is the special endowment of mystical power given to the weak. If they do not quite inherit the earth, at least they are provided with means which enable them to offset their otherwise crushing jural disabilities. With the authority which the voice of the gods alone gives, they find a way to manipulate their superiors with impunity—at least within certain limits . . . . This is broadly satisfactory to all concerned, subordinate as well as superior." *ibid.*, p. 116.

[53]Bourguignon, 1976, pp. 47–48. We could translate this into modern psychiatric terms by stating that an individual with a Dependent Personality Disorder not only gains control through his dependency, but also by his "compliance" assumes different "personalities"—thereby forming a parallel with trance possession phenomena in primitive cultures.

[54]E. Colson, *Marriage and the Family among the Platau Tonga of Northern Rhodesia*, Manchester: Manchester University Press, 1958, pp. 137ff.

[55]I. M. Lewis, *op. cit.*, p. 31.

[56]Bourguignon, *op. cit.*, p. 48.

[57]*ibid.*

[58]J. Bronowski and Bruce Mazlish, *The Western Intellectual Tradition*, New York: Harper & Brothers, 1960, p. 309.

[59]*ibid.*, p. 319.

[60]Ernest, Jones, *The Life and Work of Sigmund Freud*, Vol. 3, New York, Basic Books, 1957, p. 58.

[61]Sigmund Freud, "Contributions to the Psychology of Love: the Taboo of Virginity," in *Collected Papers*, vol. 4, New York: Basic Books, 1959, pp. 230-1.

[62]James Hillman, *The Myth of Analysis*, Evanston: Northwestern University Press, 1972, pp. 215ff. The psychiatric definition of hysteria coincides with that generally assigned to trance possession phenomena: "The mental symptoms include amnesia, somnambulisms, fugues, trances, dream-states, hysterical 'fits' or 'attacks,' etc." Leland E. Hinsle, M.D. & Robert J. Campbell, M.D., *Psychiatric Dictionary*, New York/London/Toronto: Oxford University Press, 1975, p. 367.

[63]Sigmund Freud, "Charcot," in *Collected Papers*, vol 1, New York: Basic Books, 1959, p. 20. It is important to note here, as Ellenberger points out, that by 1901 a marked decrease in hysterical phenomena occurred, "leaving it open to question whether social and cultural factors were not at work." Henri F. Ellenberger, *The Discovery of the Unconscious*. New York: Basic Books, 1970, p. 786. As early as 1859, the French physician Briquejt, in his *Traité* de l'Hystérie, determined that "hysteria was more common in the lower classes than in the higher strata of society, more frequent in the country than in the city." *ibid.*, p. 142.

[64]Sigmund Freud, "Fragment of an Analysis of a case of Hysteria," *Collected Papers*, vol. 3, New York: Basic Books, 1959, pp. 53-54, ftnote #1.

[65]Peter Homans, *Jung in Context*, Chicago/London: The University of Chicago Press, 1979, p. 138.

[66]cf. Ellenberger, *op. cit.*, "hysteria" entries, also Hillman, 1972, p. 240.

[67]Homans, *op. cit.*, p. 142.

[68]"Neurosis . . . is intimately bound up with the problem of our time. Neurosis is self-division. In most people the cause of the division is that the conscious mind wants to hang on to its moral ideal, while the unconscious strives after its—in the contemporary sense—unmoral ideal which the conscious mind . . . tries to deny. Men of this type want to be more respectable than they really are." C. G. Jung, *CW*, vol. 7, op. cit., para. 430.

[69]"By continuously expanding the recruitment of its patients, who begin as clearly characterized abnormal individuals and gradually become representative of the group, psychoanalysis transforms its treatments into conversions. For only a patient can emerge cured; an unstable or maladjusted individual can only be persuaded. A considerable danger thus arises: The

treatment (unbeknown to the therapist, naturally), far from leading to a resolution of a specific disturbance within its own context, is reduced to the reorganization of the patient's universe in terms of psychoanalytic interpretations." Claude Lévi-Strauss, *Structural Anthropology*, New York: Anchor Books, 1967, p. 178.

[70]J. A. Clausen, "The Sociology of Mental Illness," in *Sociology Today*, R. K. Merton, L. Broom, L. S. Cottrell, Jr., New York, Basic Books, pp. 485–508.

[71]"Cultural factors determine to a large extent which conditions are singled out as targets of psychotherapy and how they manifest themselves. The same phenomena may be viewed as signs of mental illness in one society, of demonical possession in another, and as eccentricities to be ignored in a third. Moreover, the behavior of the afflicted person is greatly influenced by culturally determined expectations of how persons so defined should behave." Jerome D. Frank, *Persuasion and Healing: A Comparative Study of Psychotherapy*, New York: Schocken Books, 1974, p. 318.

[72]Bourguignon, *op. cit.*, p. 8.

[73]"A neurosis is by no means merely a negative thing, it is also something positive . . . . To lose a neurosis is to find oneself without an object . . . for hidden in the neurosis is a bit of still undeveloped personality, a precious fragment of the psyche lacking which a man is condemned to resignation, bitterness, and everything that is hostile to life . . . . The patient has not to learn *how to get rid of his neurosis*, but how to bear it." C. G. Jung, *CW*, vol. 10, Princeton: Princeton University Press, 1970, pars. 355, 360.

[74]"Inasmuch as a man is merely collective," he can be changed by suggestion to the point of becoming—or seeming to become—different from what he was before. But inasmuch as he is an individual he can only become what he is and always was. To the extent that 'cure' means turning a sick man into a healthy one, cure is change. Wherever this is possible, where it does not demand too great a sacrifice of personality, we should change the sick man therapeutically. But when a patient realizes that cure through change would mean too great a sacrifice . . . then the doctor can, indeed he should, give up any wish to change or cure . . . . I always have a fair number of highly cultivated and intelligent people of marked individuality who, on ethical grounds, would vehemently resist any serious attempt to change them. In all such cases the doctor must leave the individual way to healing open, and then the cure will bring about no alteration of personality but will be the process we call 'individuation,' in which the patient becomes what he really is." C. G. Jung, *CW*, vol. 16, *op. cit.*, para. 11.

[75]"That leads me to something very important—the fact that a complex with its given tension or energy has the tendency to form a little personality of itself. It has a sort of body, a certain amount of its own psychology . . . . It can upset the stomach. It upsets the breathing, it disturbs the heart—in short, it behaves like a partial personality. For instance, when you want to say or do something and unfortunately a complex interferes with this intention, then you say or do something different from what you intended . . . . We really are forced to speak of the tendencies of complexes to act as if they were characterized by a certain amount of will-power . . . . Because complexes have a certain will-power, a sort of ego, we find that in a schizophrenic condition they emancipate themselves from conscious control to such an extent that they become visible and audible. They appear as visions, they speak in voices which are like the voices of definite people . . . . Complexes are autonomous groups of associations that have a tendency to move by themselves, to live their own life apart from our intentions. I hold that our personal unconscious, as well as the collective unconscious consists of an indefinite, because unknown, number of complexes or fragmentary personalities." Jung, *CW*, vol. 18, Princeton: Princeton University Press, 1976, para. 149, 150, 151.

[76]C. G. Jung, *ibid.*, para. 150. James Hillman, commenting upon Jung's "little people," has the following to say on the matter: " . . . as Jung puts it: 'The psyche creates reality every day. The only expression I can use for this activity is fantasy.' Man is primarily an imagemaker and our psychic substance consists of images; our being is imaginal being, an existence in imagination. We are indeed such stuff as dreams are made on.

"Since we can know only fantasy-images directly and immediately, and from these images create our world and call them realities, we live in a world that is neither 'inner' nor 'outer,' . . . . The psychic world is experienced empirically as inside us and yet it encompasses us with images. I dream and experience my dreams as inside me and yet at the same time I walk around in my dreams and am inside them." James Hillman, *Re-visioning Psychology*, New York/Evanston/San Francisco/London: Harper & Row, 1975, p. 25. So here we see further justification for postulating the existence of possession states in modern society. Because we move in a sea of images and imagination, then we have an obligation to the images. Quite simply, here we have an apt description of Berger's process of externalization, objectivation, and final internalization legitimated by an essentially religious move. As Berger points out, with the translation of religious realities "from a frame of reference of facticities external to the individual consciousness to a frame of reference that locates them within consciousness . . . traditional religious affirmation can now . . . symbolize . . . some realities presumed to exist in the 'depths' of human consciousness . . . . Psychologism . . . allows the interpretation of religions as a 'symbol system' that really refers to psychological phenomena." Berger, *op. cit.*, 1969, p. 167.

[77]Homans, *op. cit.*, p. 143.

INDEX

"A Child is Being Beaten" (Freud), 55 n. 6
A General Theory of Magic (Mauss), 173
A Lexicon of Alchemy (Ruland/Waite), 136
Abnormal/abnormality, 147, 154, 174
Accident, as wound, 24
Adam, 59, 60, 61, 63, 64, 65, 67, 78, 81, 136; as ego, 62, 63; as hermaphrodite, 59, 63; image of God, 63; second, 70; suicide of 62; symbolic of God's problem, 69
Adech, 126
Adler, Alfred, 160
Affective disorders, & class, 163
Afterlife, 25, 26
"Aggressivity in Psychoanalysis," (Lacan), 171
Ajna, 113, 115, 120 n. 29
Akropolis, 115
Alchemists, 7, 12, 15, 16, 26, 44, 60, 79, 80, 88, 118 n. 16, 130
Alchemy, 15, 16, 18, 29, 31, 41, 127, 128, 135; the couple in, 74; and the soul's imagination, 18; and tria prima theory, 15; as yoga, 88
Alexander the Great, as serpent, 115
Altered States of Consciousness (Tart), 167
Amnesia, post-hypnotic, 107
Amor and Psyche, 50
Anahata, 120 n. 29
Analysis, training, 156
Ancient Incubation Theory and Modern Psychotherapy, (Meier), 124, n. 81
Androgyne, 75, 92, 96, 97, 105, 107, 110, 116, 118 n. 16; activation of, 96; and archetypal, 93; as Christ, 60, 70, 93, 110; as a consciousness, 96, 113; and feminine, 101; geography of, 95; as God, 61; as marriage of opposites, 64; as Mercurius, 95, 117; and neurosis, 108; preexistent, 95; as realization, 93; as subtle body, 93; and transpersonal reality, 95; world of, 98
"An Essay on Pan" (Hillman), 55 n. 20
Anima, 106, 112, 117 n. 8, 123 n. 72; and animus, 92, 93, 94, 95, 97, 102, 105, 108, 116; as connecting link, 104; and ego, 94; imagining, 107; and men, 94, 104; and neurosis, 108; and reflection,

113; rejection of, 105; as shadow in women, 94; and women, 94
"Anima" I & II, (Hillman), 117 n. 8; 121 n. 36; 123 n. 72
Anima Mundi, 39; and philosopher's stone, 41; exists in the imaginal, 42
Animus, & anima, 92, 93, 94, 95, 97, 105, 108; and women, 94; & neurosis, 108
An Outline of Psychoanalysis, 108
Aphrodite, 51; beasts accompany, 49; & castration, 48, 49; & compulsion, 50; mistress of Ares, 49; mother of fear & terror, 49; murderous passion of, 49; psyche ridden by, 49, 50; & Virgin Mary, 49
Archei, 15
Archetype/archetypal, 7, 18, 39, 40, 44, 71, 79, 82, 96, 97, 99, 109, 110, 111, 118, 126, 151, 152, 170 n. 15; activation of, 96; active imagination, 44; autonomy of, 154; & body, 22; & collective unconscious, 151; connections, 42; definition of, 30; development and differentiation, 154; differentiation from, 165; divisiveness, 166; & ego, 95; & feminine, 79; hero-, 95; & horoscope, 40, 43, 47; humanizing of, 39; identification with, 171; imagining, 53; their individuation, 154; of inferiority, 80; are institutionalized roles, 152; & Kronus, 36; -language, 31; life, 31; matter, 79; meaning, 43; & Mercurius, 95; mother-, 95; & natural attitude, 152, 154; of normalcy, 152, 164; obsession by, 151, 152, 154, 155; & pathology, 154; as pattern of action, 152; phantasy-image, 123 n. 67; Philosopher's Stone, 41; protection from, 165; psychological, 31; role(s), 145, 150, 164; seeing, 31; & society, 150; soul, not property of, 39; element of spirit, 133; not static, 154; & synchronicity, 118; -wholeness, 40, 43, 47; & transformative process, 110; & zodiac, 41, 43
Archeus, 13, 125, 126, 127
Ares, see Mars
Aristotle, element theory of, 14
Ashmole, Elias, 41
Asiyah, 104
Asklepios, as serpent, 115
Astrology, 19, 20, 21, 26, 37, 38, 40, 43, 47, 126; as counselling, 31; danger for, 54; & four element theory, 14, 26; natal chart, 40; & wholeness, 41, 43
Astronomy, 126

Athena, 112, 113, 116, 170; & serpent, 115
Atlas, 53
Augustus, as serpent, 115
Avicenna, 12
Avidya, as earth, 88
Ayyangar, T. R. Srinivasa, 121 n. 31

Bacchus, 114
Barnes, Djuna, 87
"Beauty and the Beast," 169
Berger, Peter, 142, 168, 169, 176
Bios, & soul, 58
Bloom, Leopold, 97
Body, 22, 25, 80, 84, 94, 104, 111, 113, 126, 127; & archetypal, 22; as earth, 100; & ego, 41; as erotegenic zone, 108; four humours of, 15; freed by alchemy, 137; & Gods, 22; healed, 20; as hermaphrodite, 93; & illness, 15; imaginal, 110; & imagination, 136; medicine of, 127; & psyche, 23, 127; & sefiroth, 60; & soul, 15, 80; & sulpher-mercury, 15; a temple, 26; transpersonal, 110
Body, subtle, 20, 25; as androgyne, 93, 95; not created, 26; creation of, 47; & death, 41; as Philosopher's Stone, 42; & wholeness, 41; world of, 101
Bombast, Georg, 11
Bone, eternal & divine, 63; as feminine principle, 63
Book of Adam & Eve, 62
Bourguignon, Erika, 157, 163, 164, 171, 173, 175
Brahma, 113, 114
Bronowski, J., 173
Broom, L., 175
Brown, J.A.C., 123 n. 71
Buddha, 24
Calendar, seasonal & astronomical, 32ff
Campbell, Joseph, 121 n. 31
Campbell, Robert J. 174
"Cancer in Myth & Dream" (Lockhart), 137
Casey, Edward S. 55 n. 21
Castration, 36; and Aphrodite, 48; -complex, 160; and ego, 36
Celsus, 12
Chakra(s), 100, 102, 105, 109, 112, 113, 115, 120 n. 29; inverted in West, 106
"The Chakras of Kundalini Yoga," 120 n. 29
"Charcot," (Freud), 174
Chavvah, 77
Chayyah, 77
Chemistry, 13, 18

China, 77
Christ, 24; as androgyne, 60, 70, 93, 110; God as, 70; imitation of, 23; as Philosopher's Stone, 60
Christianity, 60, 111, 158; as cult, 172
Christou, Evangelous, 96, 118 n. 17
Class, & hysteria, 174; & pathology, 163; & schizophrenia, 163
Clausen, J. A., 175
Coercion, & Freud, 142, 143, 144; & natural attitude, 152; & pathology, 152
Collected Dialogues of Plato, 56 n. 30, 138
Colson, E., 173
Complex, 164; ego as, 41; has ego, 175; as little personality, 41, 175; mother-father, 41; willpower of, 175
Compulsion, & Aphrodite, 50; & Kronos, 49; & sexuality, 48; of Uranos, 51; value in, 49
Conjunction, with the feminine, 84
Consciousness, 33, 39, 42, 44, 46, 52, 53, 67, 69, 94, 97, 98, 99, 100, 105, 111, 112, 117, 122 n. 53, 124 n. 86, 129, 134, 147ff, 149, 151, 158, 167, 176; refers to, 139–140; altered states of, 141, 156; & androgyne, 93, 96, 99, 113; controls, 24; cult of, 162; as desert, 63; differentiated, 93; dissociation of, 161; divinity of, 61; ego, 42, f63, 95; extension of, 87; extinction of, 93; fragile & limited, 140; hermaphrodite as symbolic of, 59, 92, 93; & image, 98; & instinct, 134; Kronian, 47; & libido, 44; limit of, 52; as masculine, 33, 34, 103; of the natural attitude, 149; & normalcy, 152; as normality, 163; & opposites, 61, 64, 92, 93, 117; personified in myth, 32; as possession, 149; origins in projections, 143; & psychic processes, 134; & reality, 166; & reflection, 102, 121 n. 36; Saturn &, 36, 37, 52; as serpent, 64, 65; & separation, 92; & Shiva-Shakti, 101, 111; as sin, 62; as social phenomenon, 141; & society, 168; & Sol/sun, 35, 92; solar and lunar, 71, 88; soul won by, 63; & spirit, 134; & suffering, 70; & synchronicity, 96; & *themistes*, 151; Uranian, 47
"Contributions to the Psychology of Love: the Taboo of Virginity," (Freud), 174
Copernicus, 16
Corbin, Henri, 30, 54 n. 2, 96, 98, 118 n. 15, 119 n. 22, 127
Cornford, Francis Macdonald, 138
Corpus Hermeticum (Scott), 56 n. 23

Cottrell, Jr., L.S., 175
Counselling, 39, 40, 43, 45; dangers of Saturnian, 47; & Saturn, 31, 49
Creation, 92; grossest part of, 76; Hindu, 66, 77; imagination &, 67; myths & neurosis, 108; seven days of, 71; Winnebago myth, 65ff
Creation Myths, (von Franz), 117
Creative Imagination in the Sufism of Ibn 'Arabi (Corbin), 119 n. 22
The Crisis of European Sciences & Transcendental Phenomenology, (Husserl), p. 167
The Crow, 85
Cult(s), & affliction, 157; & Christianity, 158; -of consciousness, 162 founding members of, 156; healing-, 157, 162; as legitimate institution, 156; permanent & institutional, 156; possession- & class, 157; promote self-esteem, 158; socially sanctioned, 156
Culture & Depression: Studies in the Anthropology & Cross-Cultural Psychiatry of Affect and Disorder, (Kleinman & Good), 172
Cupid, 108
Cure, 22, as change, 175; too great a sacrifice, 175
Cyclopes, 32
Daemons, 16
Death/dying, 25; denial of, 25; & initiation, 172; & Nature, 26; as process, 25; & skeleton, 63; & soul, 48, 53; soul & spirit connected by, 134; & subtle body, 41; Tree of Knowledge &, 64; & water, 48
"Deautomatization & the Mystic Experience," (Deikman), 167
Deikman, Arthur, J., 167, 173
Deimos, & Aphrodite, 49
Delos, 114
Demeter, 32
Depression, function of Saturn, 48
"Depression, Buddhism, and the Work of Culture in Sri Lanka," (Obeyesekere), 172
Desert, as consciousness, 63; & soul, 63
"The Development of the Sexual Function" (Freud), 123 n. 64
Deviance; A Cross-Cultural Perspective, (Edgerton), 171
Deviant, 147; & norm, 144
"The Devouring Father" (Stein), 55 n. 11
Dionysus, 115, 116; & phallus, 114
Dionysus: Myth & Cult (Otto), 124 n. 80

Disassociation, of consciousness, 161; & gods, 150; inherent in psyche, 150
The Discovery of the Unconsciousness (Ellenberger), 122 n. 55
Disease, 23, 25; aestheticism of, 21; & Gods, 22, 23; Paracelsus' theory of, 13, 15
Dissolution, of Nature, 26
Dream(s)/dream interpretation, 127, 146, 170, 176
"The Dream and the Underworld" (Hillman), 54 n. 3
"The Dream Life of a Primitive People: The Dreams of the Vir Voron of Australia," (Schneider & Sharp), 170
Dunham, H. Warren, 171
Earth, 84; as chakra, 106; body &, 80, 100; as female, 33, 104; feminine housed in, 105; as Great Mother, 33; as ignorance, 88; as Kabbalistic Kingdom, 76; life is, 48; as Malkuth, 76; soul trapped on, 63; water & 48
Ecstatic Religion, (Lewis), 173
Eden, 62, 69; wife of Elohim, 103
Edgerton, Robert B., 171
Edmund Husserl: Philosopher of Infinite Tasks (Natanson), p. 168
Ego, 37, 42, 46, 87, 104, 111, 112; Adam as, 62, 63; angelology of, 26; & archetype, 95; & castration, 36; as complex, 41, 42; & consciousness, 41, 63, 95, 97; defenses, 134; differentiation of, 63; diminutive, 62; dry, 48; -world, 99; as idealized center, 42; Kronus &, 34; & libido, 108; male, 94; as masculine, 34; & Paradise, 63; primitive aspects of, 46; & reflection, 102; & self, 112; & Shiva, 103; subtle body, 41; young, 62
Elements, & astrology, 26; four humours & tempers of, 14; soul of, 15
Eliade, Mircea, 71, 110, 123 n. 68, 172
Ellenberger, Henri F., 122 n. 55, 174
Elohim, creator of universe, 103; husband of Eden, 103
Embryogenesis (Grossinger), 7
Empiricism, 39
The Epistles of Ali Puli, (Hamilton-Jones), 137
Eros, 38, 109, 114; compulsion & 51; as Freudian libido, 108; & moon, 101; in muladhara, 108; & psyche, 49, 50
Erotogenic, zones, 108, 109
Essays on a Science of Mythology, (Jung/Kerenyi), 117
Eve, 59, 61, 62, 64, 76, 78, 81; & con-

sciousness, 65; & serpent, 61; as soul, 63
Exhalations, 15
Externalization, 176; outpouring of human
being, 168
Facing the Gods, (Hillman), 171
Fairytales, 85, 86; & socialization, 169
Father, as heaven, 60; and hermaphrodite,
60
Feeling, 127
Female, 59, 88, 94, 111; as counterpart,
75; earth as, 53; psyche as, 85; rejection of, 105
Feminine, 33 ff, 59, 60, 63, 78ff, 80, 83,
84, 87, 88, 105, 106, 111, 112, 116, 124
n. 86; androgyne &, 101; assumptions
regarding the, 169; as bone, 63; conjunction with, 84; debased, 78; divine,
77; & earth, 77, 104, 105; exalted, 75;
exiled, 76, 80; existence &, 79; inferior,
60, 110; Kronos limits, 49; & masculine,
86, 93; & matter, 79, 80; & men, 33, 34,
86; prisoner, 77; queenly aspects of, 84;
reflective, 112, 113; rejected, 79; relationship to, 74; shakti, 95; as soul, 63;
& transformation, 81; unconscious as,
103
Folktales, & socialization, 169
Foucault, Michel, 167
"Fragments of an Analysis of a case of
Hysteria," (Freud), 174
Frank, Jerome D., 175
Freeman, Kathleen, 56 n. 25 & 31
Freud & the Post-Freudians (Brown), 123
n. 71
Freud, Sigmund, 33, 34, 36, 55 n. 6, 80,
108, 109, 110, 112, 122 n. 56, 58, 123
n. 71, 142, 143, 152, 153, 155, 160, 165,
168, 171, 173, 174; & hypnosis, 107; &
imagination, 107; & myth of the un-
conscious, 107
From Primitives to Zen (Eliade) 71 n. 3 & 4
The Future of an Illusion, (Freud), 168
Gaia, 32
Galen, 12, 14, 15
Galenic theory, 15
Galileo, 16
*The Game of Wizards: Psyche, Science,
& Symbolism in the Occult* (Poncé),
p. 54, n. 5
Genesis, 59, 66, 68, 69; continuance of,
47; God of, 61, 65; & hermaphrodite,
93; & imagination, 128; second, 62; the
work of, 45
Genitals, 76, 93, 106, 109, 110, 113; & un-
conscious, 106

Gibbons, Don C., 171
The Glass Axe, 83
Gloria Mundi, 131
Gnosticism, its founding, 172; of Justin,
103; of Simon, 104; & Sophia, 104
Gnosticism & Early Christianity (Grant),
121 n. 44
God(s) 74, 111, 125, 128, 136; Adam as
image of, 63; androgynous, 61; appre-
hension of, 45; of astrology, 38; Christ
as, 70; & dissassociation, 150; & disease, 22, 23, 47, 64; in evolution, 45;
& feminine, 76; of Genesis, 61, 65; Hermaphrodite created by, 61; & imagination, 67; individuation of, 45; loneliness
of, 65ff; & opposites, 68; as psychic factors, 30; image of self, 63; & serpent,
65; unconscious, 67, 68; unity of, 68;
wounded, 23
The Gods of the Greeks, (Kerenyi), 170
Gold, 29, 132, 133; found in filth, 79
Good, Byron, 172
Grant, Robert M., 121 n. 44
Greeks, 16, 151
The Greeks & their Gods (Guthrie), 124
n. 83
Grossinger, Richard, 7
Guthrie, W.K.C., 124 n. 83

Hades, 32, 53, 54, 134
Hamilton-Jones, W., 137
Harrison, Jane, 150, 170
Hartmann, Franz, 27 n. 1 & 3, 136
Head, contains Shiva, 103
Healer/healing, 144; coercive, 144; defini-
tion of, 144; metaphysic of, 144
Heart, emotion & intuition of, 63
Heaven, as father, 60; & hermaphrodite,
60; imagination &, 41, 42, 46; & lead
of, 52; of Paracelsus, 46; of the soul, 52
Hephaestus, 49
Hera, 32
Heraclitus, 48, 52, 53, 58
Hermaphrodite, 92, 99, 117; Adam as, 59,
93; asexual, 60; as body, 93; in Chris-
tianity, 60; God created, 61; in Judaism,
60; as Mercurius, 95; & neurosis, 108;
& opposites, 60; Paradise of, 98; transformation of, 95; unconscious of, 61,
64, 92, 93; undivided, 92
Hermes, 116; & phallus, 114; & unconscious, 114; & underworld, 114
*The Hermetic & Alchemical Writings of
Paracelsus* (Waite), 27 n. 2 & 6, 55 n.
12, 136, 138

Hermetica (Scott), 45, 129, 131, 137
Hermetic Museum (Waite), 89, 137, 138
Hesiod, 32, 48, 49, 52, 53
Hestia, 32
Hiranyagarbha, 100
Hillman, James, 43, 44, 46, 53, 54 n. 3, 55 n. 16, 55 n. 20, 62, 71 n. 1, 82, 89 n. 2, 94, 95, 114, 116, 117 n. 18, 121 n. 36 & 37, 123 n. 66 & 72, 124 n. 78 & 85, 160, 170, 174, 176
Hinsle, Leland E., 174
History, Kronus as archetype of, 36
Hollingshead, August B., 171
Homans, Peter, 174, 177
The Homeric Gods (Otto), 123 n. 73
Horoscope, 45, 46; as active imagination of Gods, 45; & archetypal imagination, 45; & archetypal wholeness, 40; the imaginal, 42; soul's expression of itself, 26
Hsu, Francis L. K., 171
Humours, four, 14; & body, 15; governed by planets, 15; Paracelsus' theory of, 15
Husserl, Edmund, 167
Hypnosis, & amnesia, 107; & Freud, 107
"Hypnosis & the Concept of the Generalized Reality-Orientation," 167
Hysteria, 160, 161, 174; definition of, 174; & possession, 161
"Hysterical Phantasies & their Relations to Bisexuality" (Freud), 122 n. 56

Iatrochemists & iatrochemistry, 15, 16
Ibn 'Arabi, 58
Ida, 101, 120 n. 29, 121 n. 31
The I Ching or Book of Changes (Wilhelm/Baynes), 119 n. 20
Illness, 15, 18, 23; & God, 22, 47; mental, 13; metaphors of, 23
Image, 126, 127, 129, 130, 134; concretized, 62; & consciousness, 44, 98; of God, 63; of the horoscope, 45; & libido, 144; & myth, 38, 39; & sleep, 53; of the soul, 75; transformation of, 44, 58
Imaginal, 17, 18, 45, 47, 52, 74, 106, 107, 128, 129, 131; & androgyne, 99; dimension, 43; geography, 130, 131; horoscope, 42; & imagination, 42; intrusions of, 135; of Paracelsus, 46; & pathology, 99; - & transpersonal body, 111; work, 43
Imagination, 17, 18, 20, 40, 59, 106, 111, 129, 130, 134, 136; active, 44, 45, 67, 119 n. 22; archetypal, 44, 46, 53; astrology born of, 20; Creation, 67; created

by death, 134; & Freud, 107; & Genesis, 128; & the Gods, 38; heaven created by, 42; & horoscope, 45, 46; as illumination, 134; imaginal composed of, 42; as Mercury, 133; organ of, 98; & Philosopher's Stone, 41; & prayer, 128; & soul, 26, 43, 134; & spirit, 126, 133; as star, 126; & transformation, 58; is transorgan, 127; as visual dialogue, 128; world created by, 101; & yoga, 101
Individual, 149; enemy of civilization, 142; & nomos, 148; & reality-frame breakdown, 156; & roles, 145; socialization of, 146; & value system, 146
Individuation/individuating, 147, 175; & archetypes, 154; of the Gods, 45; & Gnosticism, 172; & normalizing psychology, 165; & personality, 164; point of, 165; -psychology, 165; & rigid persona, 165; society's, 155; unconscious process, 154
Industrial Revolution, 158, 161, 162
Initiation, 83; ceremonies, 172; & possession-trance illness, 164; & the shaman, 172; & sickness vocation, 172
Instinct(s), 83, 102, 133; coercion of, 141; & compulsion, 44; & consciousness, 134; in Freudian psychology, 108; in Jungian psychology, 101; & Kronos, 49; of non-human world, 142; organization of, 153; reflective, 102; repression of, 153; as serpent, 65; & sublimation, 153; value in, 49
Institutions, define roles, 145, 151; & natural attitude purpose of, 146
Intellect, 127
Internalization, 143, 145, 168, 176; of society, 146
Introduction to Tantra Shastra (Woodroffe), 120 n. 28
Introduction to the Work of Marcel Mauss, (Levi-Strauss), 171
Introspection, 145, 146
Ishshah, 77

Jabir ibn Hayyan, 14, 15
James, William, 97, 118 n. 18, 128, 137
Jones, Ernst, 173
Jones, Joseph F., 171
Joseph Karo: Lawyer & Mystic, (Werblowsky), 137
Joyce, James, 96
Judaism, 60
Jung, Carl, 22, 23, 24, 27 n. 5, 30, 35, 37, 38, 39, 41, 42, 44, 47, 53, 54 n. 1 & 4,

55 n. 8–10, 15, 19 & 22, 56 n. 24, 28 & 29, 71 n. 2, 92, 93, 94, 95, 96, 98, 101, 102, 104, 105, 106, 111, 112, 115, 117 n. 1–8, 118 n. 11–16, 119 n. 21, 22, & 23, 121 n. 34, 36, 37, 42, 43, & 46, 122 n. 49 & 54, 123 n. 67, 69, & 70, 127, 133, 137, 138, 146, 149, 150, 151, 152, 154, 155, 161, 164, 165, 169, 170, 172, 174, 176; *Collected Letters of*, 117 n. 6, 118 n. 13, 119 n. 22; *Collected Works of*, 27 n. 5, 54 n. 1 & 4, 55 n. 8–10, 15, 19, & 22, 56 n. 28 & 29, 71 n. 2, 117 n. 2–5 & 7, 118 n. 11–12, & 14–16, 119 n. 21 & 23, 121 n. 34, 37, 42, 43 & 46, 123 n. 67, 69 & 70
Jung in Context, (Homans), 174
Justin, Gnosticism of, 103

Kabbalism, 60, 75, 105, 110; four worlds of, 104
Kalpana, 101
Kama, 100
Kama-Kala-Vilasa (Woodroffe), 76, 119 n. 25
Kellipoth, 76
Kerenyi, Karl, 82, 89 n. 1, 117, 150, 151, 170
Kether, & soul, 76
Kleinman, Arthur, 172
Knight, Richard Payne, 124 n. 79
Krishna, Gopi, 121 n. 31
Kronos, see Saturn
Kundalini, 103, 104, 105, 112, 113, 115, 120 n. 29, 121 n. 31, 122 n. 54; & lingam, 61, 106; & serpent of Genesis, 64; as Shakti, 100; -yoga, 95
Kundalini: The Evolutionary Energy in Man (Krishna), 121 n. 31
Kundalini Yoga (Pandit), 120 n. 29, 121 n. 41

Lacan, J., 171
Law, William, 136
Lead, alchemical 29; key of heaven, 52, resolves imperfections, 52; Saturn as synonym for, 29
Leibniz, 74
Levi-Strauss, 153, 155, 171, 172, 174
Lewis, I. M., 173
Libido, 108, 109; apprehended by the image of, 44; & ego, 108; as Eros, 108; Freudian theory of, 108
The Life & Work of Sigmund Freud, (Jones), 173
Lindsay, Jack, 56 n. 27

Lingam, 120 n. 29, & kundalini, 61
Lockhart, R. A., 127, 137
Logos, & sun, 101
The Logos of the Soul (Christou), 118 n. 17
Loneliness, God's, 65ff; Shiva &, 77
Love, & Aphrodite, 49; born of castration, 48; & Kronian blindness, 49
Lucretius, 49
Luna, 78; as unconscious, 35

Macrocosm, 100
Mahabramananda, 100
Male, 59, 86, 88, 94; ego, 94; as Great Father, 33; psyche, 85; as sky, 33
Malkuth, as earth, 76; as Kingdom, 76
Mana, skeleton as -object, 63
Manipura, 120 n. 29
Marriage, Sacred, & Mercurius, 95, 117; of the sun and moon, 71
Marriage & Family and the Family among the Platua Tonga of Northern Rhodesia, (Colson), 173
Mars, 19; & Aphrodite, 49
Masculine, 35ff, 59, 60, 85, 87, 88, 106, 116; assumptions regarding, 169; & Athena, 113; consciousness as, 33, 103; & feminine, 86, 93; fixity of, 104; reconciliation with, 84; & reflection, 113; serpent as, 115; as spirit, 81; superiority, 74, 110; tyrannical, 60; & unconscious, 33; & yang, 95
Matter, 80; is feminine, 79, 80; & Uranos, 47
Mauss, Marcel, 173
Mazlish, B., 173
Mead, George Herbert, 168
Medicine, 15, 18, 26; of the body, 127; of the soul, 127
Medusa, 113
Meier, C. A., 124 n. 81
Meister Eckhart, 52
Mental illness, as distress, 163; as metaphorical disease, 158; signs of, 175; & social class, 153
"Mental Illness, Biology and Culture," (Wallace), 171
Mercurius, as androgyne, 95; as archetypal reality, 95; as collective unconscious, 95; as conjunction, 117; as hermaphrodite, 95; sacred marriage occurs in, 95
The Meridian Handbook of Greek Mythology (Tripp), 124 n. 84
Mercury, as alchemical tree, 132, 133; as

imagination, 133; treatment for syphilis, 12
Merton, R. K., 175
Meru, Mt., 100
Metis, 32, 37, 112; aspect of soul, 52
Microcosm, 100
Mind, 126, 130; healed by heavens, 20; & social environment, 167
"Models of Madness," (Szasz), 169
Moon, -channel, 101
Mother, 84; as earth, 60; & hermaphrodite, 60
Mother, Great, myths of and calendar, 32; as personification, 33
Muladhara, 100, 105, 112, 113, 120 n. 29, 122 n. 49 & 53; as earth, 106; contains eros, 108
"Mundus Imaginalis or the Imaginary & the Imaginal" (Corbin), 54 n. 2, 118 n. 15
The Myth of Analysis (Hillman), 123 n. 66, 124 n. 85, 174
Myth/mythology, 38ff, 83, 112; collective, 167; Freudian, 110; & geographic points, 131; Greek, 150; Horoscope as continuation of, 45; & individuating therapies, 167; & normalizing therapies, 167; & psychology, 30; of unconscious, 107
Myths and Symbols in Indian Art and Civilization (Zimmer), 123 n. 74

Natal chart, 40
Natanson, Maurice, 168
Natural attitude, 141, 146, 147, 148, 149, 153, 167; & archetype, 152, 154; & coercion, 152; consciousness of, 149; defined by, 146; & individuating perspective, 166; & norm, 152; one-dimensional, 147; as real, 142; roles & institutions, 146; & sacrifice, 164; & therapy, 149; as unconsciousness, 149
Nature, 25, 82, 130; & archetypes, 39; & death, 26; dissolution of, 26; illuminating principle of, 125; occult virtue of, 126; spirit in, 64; untamed, 102; the work of, 44
Neumann, Erich, 34, 55 n. 7
Neurosis, 108, 122 n. 58, 160; & normalizing therapies, 165; as a point in life, 164; positive, 22, 175; as possession, 164; as self-division, 174; should not get rid of-, 175; symptoms, 122 n. 56; as undeveloped life, 164; undeveloped personality, 175

The New Pearl of Great Price, (Waite), 137
Nigredo, 134
Nomos, 140, 146ff., 148; social, 162; & social institutions, 151; well-defined, 146
Normal/normalcy/norm(s), 146, 146, 148, 154, 162, 166; archetype of, 152, 164; & consciousness, 152; definition of, 144; established, 144; guidelines of, 166; & the individual, 147; & individuating psychology, 165; & natural attitude, 152; & normalizing psychology, 165; & possession, 164; & projections, 145; & religious scripture, 143; & society, 152
Nu-chieh, 77
Numinosity, & institutionalized necessities, 152; & social institutions, 151

Obeyeshere, Gananath, 172
Objectivations, 145, 168, 176
Oceanus, 52, 112
Ochsner, Elsa, 11
Oedipus, 36, 110
"On the Necessity of Abnormal Psychology: Ananke & Athene," (Hillman), p. 170
"On the Significance of the Indian Tantric Yoga" (Zimmer), 121 n. 31
Opposites, 23, 46, 61, 71, 75, 111, 119 n. 21; androgyne as marriage of, 64; in China, 76ff; conflict of, 70; & consciousness, 93; God composed of, 68; & hermaphrodite, 60, 93; & human condition, 61; reconciliation of, 106
Olympus, 46
On the Nature of Things (Lucretius), 49
Organs, 21; soul expressed through, 26
The Origins & History of Consciousness (Neumann), 55 n. 7
The Origins of Alchemy in Graeco-Roman Egypt (Lindsay), 56 n. 27
Orpheus, 114
Osiris, 114
Otto, Walter, 113, 123 n. 73, 124 n. 77 & 80
An Outline Of Psychoanalysis (Freud), 122 n. 59

Pan, 38, 115, 116; & phallus, 114
Pan & the Nightmare, Two Essays (Hillman), 55 n. 20, 124 n. 78
Pandit, M. P., 120 n. 29
Paracelsus, 16, 17, 18, 20, 21, 26, 27 n. 1 & 2, 40, 42, 43, 55 n. 12, 55 n. 14, 125, 126, 127; birth and death of, 11;

chemical theory of humours, 15
Paracelsus: Life & Prophecies (Hartmann), 27 n. 1
Paradise, 63, 64, 70; ego and, 63; of Genesis, 59; of hermaphrodite, 68; as unconscious, 62, 63
Parashiva, 100, 112; as sun, 100
Pathology/pathological, 135, 147, 153, 172; archetypal, 154; & coercion, 152; & imaginal, 99; & possession, 162; as social posture, 163; as social state, 153; as society's process, 153
Penis-envy, 160
Perseus, 113
Persona, 165; rigid- & individuation, 165
Personality, 129, 134; -disorder(s), 165, 173; individuating, 164; new- & possession, 164; non-trance, 164; sacrifice of, 175; sacrificed to natural attitude, 164; & theory of, 143; transformation of, 127
Persuasion and Healing, (Frank), 175
"Phaedo," (Plato), 138
Phallus, 113, 120 n. 29; Greek Gods of, 114; & Kundalini, 106, 109
Pharmaceutics/pharmacology, 13, 16, 18
Philosopher's Stone, as androgyne, 60; as Christ, 60, 71; as subtle body, 42; & zodiacal archetype, 41
Phobos, & Aphrodite, 49
Pingala, 101, 120 n. 29, 121 n. 31
Planets, 20; & alchemy, 15; four humours of, 15; internal & external, 132; as Gods, 38
Plato, 53, 56 n. 30, 128, 131, 132, 134, 137
Plato's Cosmology, (Cornford), 138
Plutarch, 114
Poimandres of Hermes Trismegistus, 80
Polarities, see opposites
Poncé, Charles, 54 n. 5
Poseidon, 32
Possession, 144, 148, 176; by an archetype, 151, 152, 154; beliefs and rituals, 171; & complex, 164; cults, 155ff.; & hysteria, 161; & inflation, 171; as neurosis, 164; & new personality, 164; non-trance, 157, 158, 160, 162, 163, 166; & normalcy, 164; & oppressed groups, 157; & power, 157; as protest, 161; as psychoneuroses, 155; psychopathology &, 162; & societal demands, 155; by spirits, 157; & therapy, 164, 166; three types of societal responses to, 162; two categories of, 157, 164, 166, 173, 174; as unconscious autonomy, 155

Possession, (Bourguignon), 171
Prayer, & imagination, 128
The Pre-Socratic Philosophers (Freeman), 56 n. 25
Prince, 85
Princess, 85
Projection, 34, 70, 97, 116; as contractual agreement, 145; & consciousness, 35; of inferiority, 80; of our souls, 75; withdrawal, 98
Psyche, 17, 21, 33, 35, 37, 43, 50, 84, 96, 113, 150; & Aphrodite, 49; archetypes transcend, 38; & body, 23, 92; & body, 127; collective, 151, 154; creates reality, 176; & dissociation, 150; & Eros, 49; evolutionary, 111; God's, 65, 70; of the infant, 61; & inferiority, 80; male, 85; & reflection, 102; split- 161; & undeveloped personality, 175; as universal, 166
Psychiatric Dictionary, (Hinsle & Campbell), 174
Psychic energy, see Libido
Psychoanalysis/psychotherapy, 162, 163, 164, 174; birth of, 160; & women, 161
Psychological Anthropology, (Hsu), 171
"Psychological Commentary on Kundalini Yoga" (Jung), 122 n. 49, 170
Psychological Types (Jung), 119 n. 22, 137
Psychology, 18, 21, 37, 40, 43, 148, 152, 166; & imaginal, 99, 111; individuating, 165; as a metaphysic, 166; mythologizes reality, 167; & mythology, 30; normalizing, 165; personification in, 35; a religion, 149; separates person from cosmos, 39; society's socialization program, 149; as standard-bearer, 144
The Psychopathology of Everyday Life, (Freud), 155
Purusha, 66, 100
Putrefaction, 26

Queen, 83, 84

"The Realities of Practical Psychotherapy" (Jung), 123 n. 69
Reality/-frame(s), 167; breaking of, 141, 144, 156; challenged, 141; composition, 146; consciousness of, 166; as created by coercion, 142; definition of reality, 140; defense system of, 152; defines being-in-the-world, 143; delicate, 141; derives form from psyche, 143; established, 144; mythologized, 167; & personality, 143; rupturing of, 161; socially constructed, 147

Redlich, Fredrick C., 171
Reflection, 101, 113; & anima, 113, 121 n. 36; & Athena, 113; as instinct, 101; & masculine, 113; & psyche, 102; psychological process of, 134; as Shakti, 100
The Religions of the Greeks and Romans (Kerenyi), 89
Repression, 33, 34, 70, 80; in fairytales, 86; of instincts, 153; soul &, 79
The Republic, (Plato), 137, 138
Resurrection, & initiation, 172
Re-Visioning Psychology (Hillman), 43, 55 n. 16, 71 n. 1, 89 n. 2, 176
Rhea, 32
Roles, 154; archetypal, 164; & archetypes, 150; societal, 144, 145ff, 151, 169
Ruland the Elder, Martin, 126, 136
The Sacred and the Profane (Eliade), 123 n. 68
The Sacred Canopy: Elements of a Sociological Theory of Religion, (Berger), 168
Sacrifice, & conflict, 146; of personality, 175; too great for cure, 175
St. Ambrose, 52
Sahasrara, 120 n. 29
S'akti & S'akta (Woodroffe), 119 n. 25
Salt, 15
Satapatha Brahmana, 66
Saturn/Kronos, 19, 32, 36, 38, 46, 47, 48, 50, 54; of angelic purity, 52; archetype of history, 32; blindness of, 49; & compulsions, 49; & consciousness, 36, 37, 52; & counselling, 31; as dark purger, 52; & ego, 34; emasculated father, 32; & feminine, 49; inward and outward, 40; as lead, 29; as liberator, 47; limitation of, 51
Schizophrenia, 175; & complexes as partial personalities, 42; statistical incidence, 163
Schneider, David, 170
Scott, Walter, 56 n. 23, 137
The Secrets of Alchemy (Paracelsus), 55 n. 14
The Secret of the Golden Flower (Wilhelm/Jung), 27 n. 4, 55 n. 56
Sefiroth/Sefirothic, 60, 105, 110
Self, & ego, 103, 112; God image, 63; & unconscious, 63, 106
Self & Society, (Mead), 168
Sendivogius, 125
Serpent, 70; Alexander the Great as, 115; Asklepios as, 115; & Athena, 115; Augustus as, 115; as consciousness, 64; & Eve, 61; of Genesis, 59, 69, 115; as instinct, 65, 68; as Kundalini, 106; & Kundalini Yoga, 64; as masculine, 115; as Shakti, 100, 115; subtle, 64; & sympathetic nervous system, 64
The Serpent Power (Woodroffe), 119 n. 27, 121 n. 30 & 33
Sexual Symbolism: A History of Phallic Worship (Knight/Wright), 124 n. 79
Shakti, 75, 100, 101, 107, 120 n. 29; created thirty-six worlds, 100; feminine & yin, 95; Maya-, 101; as mirror, 77, 100; as serpent, 100, 115
Shaman/shamanism, 164, 171, 172; & cults, 155; role of, 144
Shamanism: Archaic Techniques of Ecstasy, (Eliade), 172
Sharp, Lauriston, 170
Sheehan, Prof. Donald, 50
Shekhinah, 75, 104, 105; as Earth, 76; in exile, 75; as fourth Kabbalistic world, 76; as Malkuth, 76; without soul, 76; as unconscious, 105
Shiva, 101, 113, 114, 115; alone, 77; aspect of consciousness, 111; located in head, 103; masculine and yang, 95; as Parashiva, 100; & serpent, 115
Shor, Ronald E., 167
Silver, 132, 133
Simon, 104
Sin, consciousness as, 61; of Genesis, 59
Skeleton, as feminine, 63; as *mana* object, 63
Sky, as male and Great Father, 33; as Uranos, 37
Social class, & mental illness, 153
Social Class & Mental Illness, (Hollingshead & Redlich), 171
Society/societies/societal, 166, 172; coerces individuals, 143; coerciveness of, 144; & consciousness, 147, 168; deficiency in, 146; demands imitation, 152; & the individual, 146; & individuation, 155; internalization of, 146; & the norm, 146; numinosity of, 152; & pathology, 153; & possession, 163–4; projection of psychic structures, 143; as reality, 144; roles, 144; split in, 166; success of, 145
Sociological Theory & Mental Disorder, (Dunham), 171
"The Sociology of Mental Illness," (Clausen), 175
Sociology Today, (Merton, Broom & Cottrell), 175
socialization, 169; universal, 166
Socrates, 16

Sol, 78; as consciousness, 35
Song of Solomon, 84
Sophia, 104
"The Sophic Hydrolith," (Waite), 137
Soul, 7, 16, 17, 20, 21, 25, 26, 39, 43, 47,
   54, 74, 79, 80, 83, 84, 96, 97, 98, 111,
   125, 126, 127, 128, 129, 134; & Adam,
   136; alchemy, product of, 18; & anima/
   animus, 94; Aphroditic trials of, 51; archaic, 58; archetypes not property of,
   39; ascension of, 131, 132, 134; base of,
   53; & *bios* & *zoe*, 58; & bodily impulse,
   134; and body, 15, 22, 80; conversion
   of, 128; cosmic, 100; of a culture, 24;
   & death, 48, 53; defined, 43; & desert,
   63; of elements, 15; & the erotic, 50; Eve
   as, 63; examined, 170; in exile, 63, 87;
   as feminine, 63, 81; freed by alchemy,
   137; function of, 63; heaven of, 52; image of, 48, 75; & the imaginal, 49, 132;
   & imagination, 26; incurable, 53; infirmities of, 127; inquisitiveness of, 63;
   Kabbalistic triad of, 76; & Kether, 76;
   language of, 18; liberating of, 147; as
   light, 134; & loving, 50; mediates, 63;
   medicine of, 126; Metis as aspect of, 52;
   as middleground, 43; night of, 52; organs express, 26, personifying tendency of, 36; & planetary zones, 132; projection of, 75; as reflective ground, 46;
   refusal of, 81; rejected, 79; repressed,
   79; roots of, 130; Shekhinah without,
   76; -making, 62; -work, 75; become
   spirit, 48; is spirit, 133; & spirit connected by death, 134; stable, 53; subject to spirit, 134; & Tiphereth, 76; &
   transformation, 81; turned into image,
   134; united by spirit, 126; of the universe, 66; & underworld, 53; from
   water, 48; & women, 94, 95; world-, 39;
   world- as zodiacal figure, 40
Soul, World, see Anima mundi
Spine, 100, 120 n. 29
Spinoza, 17
Spirit(s), 7, 17, 19, 21, 25, 84, 126; archetype &, 133; & body, 22; breakdowns
   of, 78; evil, 76; is imagination, 133; invisible, 126; masculine, 81; in Nature,
   64; & Saturn, 37; -possession, 171; is
   soul, 133; & soul connected by death,
   134; unites soul, 126
Spiritual Disciplines, 121 n. 31
Spiritualization, 37, 47, 48, 49, 54; &
   Kronos, 51
Stars, see Astrology

Status quo, 157, 162; agreement with, 148;
   conflict with, 146; maintaining of, 142
Stein, Murray, 36, 55 n. 11
Structural Anthropology, (Levi-Strauss),
   175
The Study of Deviance, (Gibbons & Jones),
   171
Suffering, in becoming conscious, 70; &
   disunity, 70; & initiation, 172; & trans-
   formation, 24
Sulpher-Mercury theory, 15; body com-
   posed of, 15
Sun, 126, 129, 132; central, 125; invisible,
   126; of man, 136; Parashiva as, 100; -
   channel, 100
Super-ego, born of guilt, 36; as internal
   coercion, 142, 143
Susumna, 109, 120 n. 29
Svahdhisthana, 106, 120 n. 29, 122 n. 49
Symbol, 35, 82, 83; visible sign, 82
synchronicity, 23, 24, 96, 118 n. 14
Syphilis, 12
Szasz, Thomas, 144, 158, 168

T'ai Chi, 93; & hermaphrodite, 61
Tantra, 100, 110
Tao, of heaven and earth, 119 n. 20
Tart, Charles T., 167
Tartoros, described, 52ff
Tattvas, created by Shakti, 100
Thanatos, 108
Theatrum Chemicum Britannicum (Ash-
   mole), 41
Themis, 150
Themis, (Harrison), 170
Themistes, & consciousness, 151
Theogony (Hesiod), 32
"The Theory of the Instincts" (Freud), 122
   n. 59
The Therapeutic State, (Szasz), 169
Therapy/therapies, 161, 135; as art, 149;
   & collective myths, 167; individuating-
   165, 166, 167; & natural attitude, 149;
   normalizing- 165, 166, 167; & posses-
   sion trance, 164, 165, 166; & protest-
   responses, 162; rituals of, 164
Thompson, Clara, 122 n. 59
Tiphereth, & soul, 76
"Timaeus," (Plato), 138
Titans, 32
"Toward an Archetypal Imagination,"
   (Casey), 55 n. 21
Transformation, 43, 64, 65, 70, 81, 82, 83,
   85, 91; archetypal process of, 110; &
   feminine, 81, 105; of hermaphroditic

natures, 95; of images, 44; & imagination, 58; & Kundalini, 64; of nature, 45; & serpant, 64; & suffering, 24; threefold process of, 100, 109; wounded god and, 23

Tree of Knowledge, 59, 61, 64, 65

Tree of Life, Sefirothic, 75

Tria prima, 15

Tripp, Edward, 124 n. 84

Two Essays on Analytical Psychology (Jung), 55 n. 17

"Two Posthumous Papers," (Jung), 169

Ulysses, 97

Upanishads, Yoga, 101

Unconscious, 33, 36, 42, 50, 67, 74, 80, 83, 122 n. 53, 146; & archetypes, 151; as chakra, 105; collective-, 95, 146, 147, 150, 176; is collective unconscious, 146; feminine, 103; God's, 67, 68, 70; & genitals, 106; as hermaphrodite, 60, 61; & Hermes, 114; inexhaustible, 35; Luna as, 35; in men, 33; as Mercurius, 95; myth of, 107; & opposites, 64; & Paradise, 62, 63; personal, 176; as petrifying, 113; & power, 143; representative of society, 146; & Self, 63; separation from, 63; shaped by society, 146; & Shekhina, 105; short-cut to, 44; is social reality, 150; & soul, 63; self, 106; as unreason, 140, 141; in women, 33; as the world, 70

Uranos, 32, 36, 37, 46; compulsion of, 51; & matter, 37

The Varieties of Religious Experience (James), 118 n. 18, 137

Vaughan, Thomas, 125, 126

Virgin Mary, 75, 84; & Aphrodite, 49

Vishnu, 113, 114

Visuddha, 120 n. 29

Vita Animae, 126

Vital, Hayyard, 131, 134, 137

von Franz, Maria 117

von Hohneheim, Philippus Aureolus Theophrastus Bombastus, 11

Waite, Arthur Edward, 27 n. 2 & 6, 136, 137

Wallace, Anthony, F. C., 171

Water, death to souls, 48; from earth, 48; metallic, 89

The Western Intellectual Tradition, (Bronowski & Mazlish), 173

Wholeness, 82; archetypal, 43, 47; astrological, 41, 43; & dark night of the soul, 52; life as, 23

Wilhelm, Richard, 27 n. 4, 56 n. 24, 119 n. 20

Witchdoctor, role of, 144

Woman, 74, 77, 86; disregard of, 75; theory of, 74

Woodroffe, Sir John, 119 n. 25-27, 120 n. 28

The Works of Jacob Behme, (Law), 136

The Works of Thomas Vaughan, (Waite), 136

World(s), as feminine, 76; four of Kabbalism, 104; fourteen of Kundalini yoga, 100; & imagination, 101; -parents, 92; as Shakti, 77; as Shekhinah, 76; thirty-six created by Shakti, 100; three, 76; transparent part of, 82

Wound/wounding, 12, 22; & accident, 24; as archetypal moment, 24; & Christ, 23; exiles us, 24; gods come to us through, 22; image of, 21; love-, 50; & soul, 24; soul message, 23

Wright, Thomas, 124 n. 79

Yang, 88; & hermaphrodite, 61; light & positive, 76; masculine & Shiva, 95; & sexuality, 77

Yesod, 106; & soul, 76

Yin, 75, 88; dark & negative, 76; feminine & Shakti, 96; & hermaphrodite, 61; & sexuality, 77

Yoga, alchemical, 88; & imagination, 101; Kundalini-, 95, 101, 109, 110, 111, 113; Tantric, 61

The Yoga Upanishad (Ayyangar), 121 n. 31

Yoni, 120 n. 29

Zambes valley, & Tonga women, 157

Zeus, 32, 38, 52, 112, 113, 115

Zimmer, Henrich, 120 n. 29, 121 n. 31, 123 n. 74

Zodiac, 43; zodiacal archetype & Philosopher's Stone, 41; zodiac & world soul, 40

Zoe, & soul, 58